P9-DUE-782

Repetition and Semiotics: Interpreting Prose Poems

REPETITION AND SEMIOTICS
INTERPRETING PROSE POEMS

by

Stamos Metzidakis

SUMMA PUBLICATIONS, INC.
Birmingham, Alabama
1986

Library of Congress Catalog Number 86-60801
ISBN 0-917786-41-6

Printed in the United States of America

ACKNOWLEDGEMENTS

This book could simply not have been written had I not benefitted as a graduate student from the knowledge and perceptive criticisms of Professor Michael Riffaterre of Columbia University. Thanks to his instructive remarks, I was able to avoid many significant mistakes and dangers intrinsic to such a study.

I would also like to thank Professor Ross Chambers of the University of Michigan, and Professor Julia Kristéva of the Université de Paris, VII (Jussieu), who, on several different occasions, provided me with invaluable suggestions for strengthening various parts of the book.

In addition to these individuals, I should also like to express my appreciation to the Faculty Research Grants Committee, as well as to the entire Graduate School of Arts and Sciences of Washington University in Saint Louis, for their financial support of the research, and publication costs of this project. In particular, the chairman of Romance Languages and Literatures, James F. Jones, Jr., and former chairman, John L. Grigsby, deserve special mention for their continued help and encouragement throughout the writing of my book.

Finally, I must express my greatest thanks to my wife Sara, whose knowledge of style is surely superior to mine, and whose energy was indispensable to the project's realization.

Note

Portions of Chapter One and Chapter Four have appeared, or will appear, in modified form under the following titles: "Formal Repetition and the Perception of Literature" in *L'Esprit Créateur*, 24 (1984), pp. 49-61; "Picking Up Narrative Pieces in a Surrealist Prose Poem" in *Orbis Litterarum* (forthcoming); and "Contra Deleuze: Towards a Singular Theory of Reading" in *Romanic Review* (forthcoming).

CONTENTS

Chapter I

FORMAL REPETITION AND LITERATURE

Repetition has a bad reputation. Repetition is stasis, it is boredom, it is death, cf. Freud. For the sake of originality or difference, it must be avoided at all costs. Repetition in literature is thus to many the sign of a dull mind, and of an even duller pen. As Malherbe implied in his commentaries on the baroque poet Desportes, repetition destroys good style.[1]

Since this "evil" is found, however, in the theoretical works of thinkers from Aristotle to Derrida, as well as in the literary productions of writers from the Greeks right down through the New Novelists, one has to ask whether it really deserves this bad reputation. Indeed, the entire history of rhetorical and stylistic studies would seem to underscore rather than to reject the fact that the iterative process is constitutive of the artistic work. One need only look, for instance, at the definition of repetition in a dictionary of rhetoric[2] to realize the extraordinary importance accorded this phenomenon in the classification and characterization of rhetorical tropes. Be they text-based, or reader-based, as with the current vogue, the vast majority of critical attempts to describe the literary event depend on the perception of repetitive textual traits for their epistemological grounding. Regardless of what a given critic may say about a piece of literature, he or she would be literally at a loss for words if there were no prior notation, conscious or unconscious, of formal iteration.

To clarify this point, I shall single out a poem that has generated a plethora of dissimilar interpretations, Rimbaud's celebrated sonnet, "Voyelles." Although everyone who reads this poem presumably reads the same marks on the page, no single reading seems any more satisfying than any other. The reason for this is that while each interpretation attempts to account for the curious relationships between the vowels and their corresponding colors, all of them single out different aspects of the text. These aspects fall into a global symbolic scheme that has somehow been extracted from the text. Some readers interpret Rimbaud's colors as being similar to those one can find in an actual color spectrum. Others see them as referring back to various mystical traditions which associated certain colors with certain sounds. Still others maintain that the poem's imagery derives directly from models provided by the specific Biblical text known as the *Apocalypse*. In each case, Rimbaud's sonnet is conceived of as being a copy of something else, something like a key which would unlock the otherwise hermetically sealed meaning of "Voyelles."

It is clear then that while the models selected by individual readers vary according to the makeup of their respective psyches, one thing never changes: the manner in which they arrive at their hermeneutic conclusions.[3] The new is always seen in terms of the old, the unknown in terms of the known. Repetition is that process which allows the reader to grasp any meaning whatsoever. As long as one can find models that justify seeing an object (a text), or even part of it, as a copy, one will be in a position to describe and interpret the workings of the text on that precise basis.

In this sense, any perception and subsequent comprehension of a poem resemble the perception and subsequent comprehension of any other object in the world. Confronted with something we do not yet know, we rely on the knowledge we already possess about other things in order to arrive at some type of understanding of the pheomenon under scrutiny. If, on the other hand, we resign ourselves to the simple statement that a poem appears to be totally "different," "unique," or "beyond words," then we are essentially admitting that we cannot put our finger on anything else which is *like* it. In so doing, we are in effect dismissing the possibility that someone else might know or notice something which could open up the text for more discussion. We thereby severely limit its capacity to produce meaning for us, and for other readers as well.

As a result, the student of literature must make the following choice: either he will hold dearly to his own un-articulated, purely emotive reactions, and insist that no one has the right to do otherwise with these texts; or else he will enter into a kind of communion, even within himself, with a long tradition of language uses, especially literature. This communion is one against which the present work gains a certain aesthetic and/or critical relief. To opt for the former is tantamount to reducing the text to little more than a personal fetish. Opting for the latter implies an acceptance of our earlier stance vis-à-vis repetition's centrality in the epistemological sphere.

In opting for the second, the student of literature realizes that he is using words; that is, he is expressing something in and of a medium whose units are verifiable and culturally located. These units are passed on, i.e., repeated, in copies recognizable to nearly every member of a given society. The individual who accepts repetition as the basis of understanding itself says to himself: "I (the reader) do not know all of what you (the scriptor of the text) know, but unless I am totally crazy (cf. the recent interest in schizophrenic discourse à la Artaud) we do know *something* of what the other knows. You have read certain books that I have read. You do use some of the same clichés, stereotypes, descriptive systems that I use. We can and do describe certain things in certain ways, with some variations. So the words you write to me do mean *something*. On the basis of some models (but which ones and where?) I grasp something of what you are writing. And though it may not necessarily be what you intended for me to grasp, your writing tells me something."

This does not mean that we should all agree on all the same models to the exclusion of others when we begin to analyze, comment on, or discuss a given work. Instead, what I am proposing is that we look carefully at how most critics proceed in their dealings with literature, and that we try, at least, to come up with a minimal set of models which, ideally, everyone could accept as potentially operative in the production of literary texts. Once again, my intention is not to suggest that certain models (sociological, psychoanalytic, historical, semiotic, etc.) are better or worse than others, but rather that a worthwhile project for a literary theorist would be to isolate those models which explain the linguistic heritage of the marks on the page *qua* visual and acoustic stimuli.

So while one reader will see copies of French society in Rimbaud's prose poems, and a second will prefer to emphasize how Rimbaud's words echo or repeat some of his personal interests, fantasies, and obsessions, I shall be concerned here with establishing a preliminary typology of iterative units, models-copies, that anyone knowing a particular language and literature should be able to concur governs the purely linguistic dimension of a literary work. In effect, my interpretations will consist of detailed descriptions of certain linguistic models that allow a text to function semiotically.

I hasten to add that the models advanced in my study must not be thought of as the sources or transcendent origins for the prose poems I have chosen to investigate. Rather, they are no more or less than simple reference points that have helped to guide my own personal readings. In addition, they can be potentially seen as those reference points which guided the poet in his writing and other readers in their differing responses to the same textual stimuli. By "potentially" I mean that a given textual feature may very well point to models other than the ones I mention in my study, depending on who is doing the reading or writing. But inasmuch as the initial feature itself can be minimally categorized in linguistic terms, the family of models it conjures up raises my suggested models to the status of "typical."

Thus, the question asked of textual phenomena will no longer be so much, "Which specific models have given rise to them?", as it will be, "Which specific *type* of linguistic model allows for their semiotic functioning, their functioning as signs?" If in the course of my analyses I seem to state categorically that such and such a stylistic feature is generated by the repetition of one model (and not others), it should always be remembered that the proposed model is meant to be exemplary, not exclusive. Furthermore, when I claim that a specific model is exemplary, then it is so primarily for *me*, given the limitations of my literary and linguistic competence.[4] That the particular model I select may not be exemplary for everyone does not in any way refute the existence of the category or conceptual paradigm into which it might figure. For I am arguing more for the categories of my typology than for the exact entries within them which I have determined to be at work. Any single, unified, or "correct" interpretation of the particular literary works chosen will therefore fade in proportion to our formulating a hierarchy of linguistic forms or frames within which a multiplicity of significations becomes possible. By delineating those parts of a text where either the writer or reader or both perform (s) an act of intellectual iteration, we will attempt to redeem repetition's reputation,[5] and to describe more simply with its aid some of the most dominant stylistic features of literature.

*   *   *

Many scholars agree that recurrent images, themes, words, rhymes, rhythms, and the like are among the hallmarks of literature. Yet few believe they explain all of its stylistic aspects. As Youri Lotman puts it: "Les répétitions des différents niveaux jouent un rôle déterminant dans l'organisation du texte et attirent depuis longtemps l'attention des chercheurs. Cependant la réduction de toute la construction artistique aux répétitions paraît erronée."[6]

In view of our earlier premise (to wit, that critics, regardless of interpretive strategy or ideological stance, prove their points by perceiving iteration), Lotman's last statement strikes me as being nostalgic. It is nostalgic to the extent that he seems to want us to think that something indeterminable, undefinable, *unnameable*, in a word, also goes into the construction of an artistic work. I will not speculate as to why he felt that way, but I should like to inquire into the precise fashion in which things are repeated in literary works. For one encounters a similar recurrence of elements in so-called natural language as well. Concepts like equivalences, redundancies, isomorphisms, overdetermination, economies, obsessive metaphors and images, parallelisms, and isotopies,[7] first used mainly to describe iterative aspects of historical documents, neurotic or psychotic discourses, geometric proofs, in a work, "non-literary" texts, were only afterwards adopted to their literary counterparts, presumably because the two types of writing are somehow related.

A tentative definition of the literary work is consequently indispensable to the present discussion. This provisional definition will serve as the basis for any modifications that result later on from my analyses. Let us call "literary" only those texts which, for whatever historical, cultural, or ideological reasons, have been canonized as such. We can add that owing to a traditional bias in our culture valorizing poetry over prose, literary texts are often called "artistic" or "poetic" as well, even though they do not always assume a versified form. Needless to say, this uncertainty over terminology already hints at how such labels involve the particular society or class using them more than the artistry, "poeticity," or "literariness"[8] of the works themselves. How else could the same work come to be called literary by some, and not by all?

Let us simply note that the Western, university-educated society to which the present study is directed implicitly bestows these adjectives on its cultural monuments by promulgating and commenting on them in books, articles, classrooms, libraries, and lecture halls. It follows that, when I claim a given writer has produced a literary text, for the moment I am not talking really about what he or she did, but rather about how we as a group have conceived of that piece of writing. We, in other words, are the ones who have created this hazy concept of literature from the example set by many different writers, as if all writers tried to set *an* example in picking up their respective pens! The peculiar selection of works that a large consensus deems worthy of such labels is thus more an empirical fact than a bone of contention. Literature exists, at the very least, *some* literature, but exactly how it acts on us, or we on it, remains open to question.[9]

This provisional definition has two great advantages for the theorist. First, it allows him to isolate and characterize poeticity within a specific corpus of poems before talking about it in general. It allows him to do this because in categorizing each group of equivalent forms or repeated paradigms in the chosen corpus he becomes aware of various text-specific levels on which the poetic function is operative. Recasting Jakobson's famous definition of this function in the light of our earlier arguments, we can assert the following: the perceived repetition (his word is "projection") of certain paradigms at different stages along the syntagmatic axis of a text reveals a substantial dimension of its poeticity to the reader.

Second, by establishing what is literary for a certain group of readers, i.e., academics and other scholarly types, this provisional definition might eventually aid us in constructing a pair of intimately linked typologies: one concerned with repeated reading techniques; the other with repeated writing practices. Since these classificatory systems would situate the literary phenomenon somewhere between the text and the reader, they could possibly supplement Roland Barthes's early attempt[10] to catalogue *écritures*, and thereby avoid considering the text outside of its historical context. The historical context I am referring to designates more the history of readers, writers, and texts than History or Historicity per se. I should emphasize that this essay does not so much concern itself with the historical factors that affected or caused certain iterative processes as it does with the exact linguistic processes engaged in by readers and writers themselves.

Yet even though we have provisionally accepted the existence of a special category designated "literary," we still cannot understand why the same texts always engender a host of divergent evaluations or readings, be they sociological, psychoanalytic, rhetorical, or semiotic. To recall what has already been said, let us look at how most critics, regardless of the perspective adopted, arrive at their judgments. In nearly every case, critics arrive at their conclusions on the basis of repetitive signs or signals they notice while reading. That is to say, once they start reading a text they have already presumed to be literary, they immediately attempt to pick out the repetitions in it:

> il nous suffit de déterminer le texte comme artistique pour qu'entre dans la construction la présomption de signifiance de toutes les ordonnances qui y ont place. Alors aucune répétition ne sera contingente par rapport à la structure. A partir de là, la classification des répétitions devient une des caractéristiques déterminantes de la structure du texte.[11]

It should be evident, however, that this procedure, which we ourselves are following at present, puts the proverbial cart before the horse. It sets aside the issue of what a literary text is, and instead passes directly to analyzing it as such. Selecting just those repetitions that corroborate its particular hermeneutic stance, most literary commentary ends up ignoring many other possible poetic features in a text. Meanwhile, it neglects the fact that individuals have to decide which paths or directions to take in the course of their reading in order to do it at all.[12]

But, as Nicolas Ruwet quite aptly points out: "Nous ne possédons, jusqu'à présent, aucun critère sûr qui nous permette de choisir parmi la multitude des équivalences possibles, celles qui sont réellement pertinentes dans tel poème, chez tel auteur, dans tel ou tel style."[13] In the wake of my preceding remarks, what Ruwet implies is crucial to any investigation of literature's specificity. His comment saves us from making unquestioned selections of textual repetitions by forcing us first to ascertain 1) how repetition works, 2) when repetitions occur, 3) what is repeated, and 4) why some are noticed, while others are not. Seeing how important each one of these topics is to the state of modern criticism, I propose to organize my chapters in an order that correspondes roughly to their treatment. By proceeding in this manner, I wish to demonstrate the extent to which repetition determines the behavior of both the writer and the reader.

*   *   *

The works of the three poets chosen for this essay, Baudelaire, Rimbaud, and Breton, fulfill the requirement set forth earlier for literary texts: they are accepted and treated as such by a large majority of critics, students, and professors. In addition, they provide an effective sampling—if for no other reason than the impressive number[14] of thematic, stylistic, and historical studies devoted to them—of writers working within a particular literary tradition. In many of these critical works, they are among the high points of what is referred to now as the "modernist" movement. Like all modern artists, these three merit the nomenclature by rejecting old-fashioned models or conventions, and creating new ones.

Yet, even though they perfected the hybrid literary genre known as the prose poem, there is a great paradox in this creation. The most remarkable qualities of their collections, *Le Spleen de Paris*, the *Illuminations*, and *Poisson soluble*,[15] lie precisely in the paucity of rules governing their production, and their lack of easily recognizable structuration. Indeed, unlike verse, plays, novels, many of which exhibit certain common features (even if critics do not agree on all the specifics), prose poems basically defied description until enough of them were written to allow Suzanne Bernard, in her now classic study of the genre, to talk about their evolution.[16]

Since my own description cannot precede my analysis, the only sure statement I can make at this time is that these poems display varying degrees of *readability*, from the most "prosaic" (Baudelaire) to the most nonsensical or absurd (Breton). In using this neologism my intention is to state a fact of literary history, nothing more. As in the case of literature itself, I prefer, for now at least, to give tradition the benefit of the doubt before challenging the opinions it has promoted for years. Even so, while these texts clearly afford a wide spectrum of the semantic possibilities endemic to the genre, the literary form of the poems remains marginal, and largely problematic. It seems likely then that an efficient way to deduce several "literary" criteria is to compare these particular texts *formally*.

Surprisingly enough, outside of Suzanne Bernard's study, most scholars had steered clear of the prose poem problem until Michael Riffaterre recently treated it at length in his *Semiotics of Poetry*.[17] In this book, destined to be a seminal work in the description of the genre, the prose poem serves as a kind of minimal poetic text, or "degree-zero" permitting the author to illustrate essentially Russian Formalist principles of literariness. What I plan to do by clarifying the notion of repetition is to expand upon Riffaterre's research, and show the need to ask the following question: Is what one critic means when he claims that two or more elements are repeated in a given work, the same as what someone else means when he singles out a different set of features? To ask this another way, is one set of (repeated) criteria more valid than any other when explicating a work?

My own tentative answer to this question is two-fold: yes, in regard to the dominant ideological and aesthetic forces in a specific society; no, with respect to a more personalized, individualized appreciation of literature. As long as institutions like universities, publishing houses, literary magazines and forums exist, there will be a societally determined validity in interpretation, a validity grounded like any other on formal iteration. Running contrary to this dominant intellectual current, however, is a qualitatively similar validity of individual readings which can aspire to the higher status only through its repetition, promotion, and dissemination by an ever growing community of disciples, students, and the like. Interpretation's essential strength, therefore, appears to be in its numbers.

Gilles Deleuze has pointed out that philosophers from Aristotle to Derrida have used the term "repetition," sometimes even devoted long discussions to it.[18] By tracing the course of the notion through all its myriad peregrinations, Deleuze gives us a detailed account of the premises underlying each usage. At the end of his search, he arrives at two major philosophical conceptions of repetition.[19] After further explication, these conceptions will be applied to an analysis of stylistic features. The first is based on what he calls the "identité du concept," where the set position and identity of the model/type allow its numerical re-presentation in an indefinite series of copies: "il y a répétition lorsque des choses se distinguent *in numero*, dans l'espace et dans le temps, leur concept étant le même" (*DR*, p.346). From this historically dominant point of view, a copy or token is not thought of as being distinct from the original, since it resembles it in every perceptible detail. As was put forth earlier vis-à-vis literary texts themselves, a third party, i.e., a particular individual or society with particular habits and prejudices, seems here again to have a large part in deciding whether a certain phenomenon (repetition) actually takes place or not. To express this in other terms: "The type only dictates those essential properties that its occurrences must display in order to be *judged* [emphasis mine] a good replica, irrespective of any other characteristic that they may possess" (Eco, *Theory*, p. 182). Thus, when a scholar notes repetition in a literary work he, not necessarily anyone else, has judged the copy a good replica. The scholar assumes that the feature in question belongs in a particular paradigm or conceptual category, and thereby excludes many others.

Of course, that an "originary unicity"[20] of a type or paradigm be posited in the first place points to the uncritically accepted Occidental belief in things being the same unto themselves, as in A = A. Most important for our purposes, it assumes that a speaker or writer is equivalent to the author or subject of a given utterance. This last presupposition especially forms the very foundation of the first kind of repetition. It is no accident, therefore, when Deleuze insists on the primacy of Descartes in this respect. The latter, he argues, makes a serious mistake in taking for granted common sense or "bon sens" (the exclusive property of that third party just alluded to) when he affirms his famous *cogito ergo sum*. For just who this third party is in Descartes' mind is never really resolved. His entire proof unfolds as if it were perfectly understood "ce que signifie moi, penser, être," not to mention "bon sens" (*DR*, pp. 169-75)!

But ever since Rimbaud somewhat facetiously wrote, "On me pense" instead of "Je pense,"[21] the nature of these concepts has ceased to be self-evident. Similarly, when André Breton decides at the beginning of his surrealist novel *Nadja*[22] that "Qui est-ce que je 'hante'?" is a better question than "Qui suis-je?", the pure, concrete, transcendental "I" perforce finds itself susceptible to great reappraisal. One can no longer assume that repetition is *simply* a matter of re-doing or reproducing a given object, precisely because the subject/object "I", at least, is not so simple anymore.

When we attempt to know a thing in the world, sooner or later (mainly sooner) we displace our attention from the thing itself to what it merely resembles.[23] For example, instead of saying that a rose is a rose is a rose and leaving it at that, we usually choose to define it in relation to something else: "any member of the species Rosa," "a dark pink to purplish pink," or any number of other random dictionary definitions. The quantum leap thus effectuated happens so naturally,[24] and so frequently in the Western world, that most people ignore the injustice done to the strict autonomy or identity of the object in question.[25] This proclivity to shift focus gives the impression that a thing in itself, say, a text, is never really enough for our inquisitive, appropriative eyes: that we must first somehow categorize, or otherwise tell what it is *like*, when dealing with it.

By right then, it should not surprise us when a similar jump, or act of bad faith, if you prefer, occurs in studying a literary work. Yet it does surprise me, if only because the same texts have received so many different interpretations. This situation makes me wonder finally whether anyone has truly figured out what literature *is*. It seems odd that instead of analyzing a text in and for itself, as a series of uniquely significant tracings found on pieces of paper, critics are always more anxious to show how it reflects or recovers various aspects of "ordinary" communication, and/or other texts, discourses, clichés, and stereotypes.

To my mind, this critical *modus operandi* points to a profound irony, an irony all the more striking because it subtends a society convinced of the identity of things unto themselves, of $A = A$. What I mean is this: it appears pragmatically impossible for me, as well as for most everybody, to understand an object except in terms of innumerable entities which are only like it. This hermeneutic impasse implies that we understand better the nature of object T, by setting up an equation of the type: $T = T_1 + T_2 + T_3$ ad infinitum, just as Cubism and Phenomenology did.

But what puzzles me about this way of treating a text is that critics usually end up learning more about themselves than about their object of study. Perhaps because we all fall prey to what Freud called our repetition-compulsion or death instinct, critics are condemned, as it were, to return to certain anterior responses to the world of literature, and thus to delimit arbitrarily, i.e., subjectively, the virtually infinite complexity of a text. So in place of the text they put their own subjectivity, their own family romances and obsessions.[26] This hypothesis is extremely tempting inasmuch as when we figure out how we want to utilize, talk about, or exchange a text in our society, we choose the function it will have for us.[27] We, the third party, decide upon its relevant aspects in order that we might know not only what it replicates, and how to use it, but also, literally, what it itself is. We thereby reduce it to a copy possessing primarily those traits T_1, T_2, T_3, which the group to which we belong agrees are in fact pertinent to its specific societal function. From this same perspective, however, any text T theoretically possesses traits T_4, T_5, etc., that are never known since they are not recognized to exist by a majority of readers. In other words, they are not emphasized by a particular culture, presumably because they are of little or no use to it. Copies or tokens can thus "possess individual characteristics, provided that they respect the *pertinent* ones fixed by the type" (Eco, *Theory*, p. 182, emphasis mine).

This statement poses two interrelated problems. First, the more intricate an object is on the empirical level, the more elusive are all of its "individual characteristics." Second, as far as our understanding of it is concerned, we have to increase substantially the number of things (models) to which this intricate object is referred or compared. Unfortunately, it does not suffice to say that "the principle of duplication does not change; what changes is the number of rules and the technical difficulties" (Eco, *Theory*, p. 181). When dealing with a complex entity with numerous traits of its own, it would appear rather that the copy is "as much original as its model" (Eco, *Theory*, p. 181). This is just another way of admitting that while knowing and reproducing toys, shirts, or money are relatively easy tasks, we cannot say as much about the stylistic features within literary texts. After all, given the enormous quantity of conflicting commentary on what are their pertinent or idiosyncratic aspects, we are probably still quite ignorant of several dimensions of their specificity, their literariness.

Maybe then the time has come to delay comparing the text to well-defined, socially accepted and known models outside its own margins until reassessing it on its own terms as well. Since a text is never known until it is read, spoken of, or written about (and because that fact presupposes not only the text's uniqueness, but also the heterogeneous knowledge brought to it by each individual reader), both factors are certainly always operative in each reading act. By recognizing the relevance to textual analysis of these two factors, we can avoid reducing the text to just another, albeit highly sophisticated, object with a cultural exchange value. In the process, it might come to be used not only as a vehicle by which a culture protects and sustains itself, but also as an epistemological tool helping us better understand how we know what we know, how we "read" the world.[28]

Thus, instead of acting as if the problem of literature were already solved, I think we can put it into a new light by: 1) scrutinizing those types of readings based on a Saussurean model, which are caught in a "prison-house of language,"[29] and 2) attempting to classify the multifarious ways by which a text repeats several different linguistic models. While it is true that much of a literary work's style can be explained in terms of stylistic models used by other writers, one can also legitimately argue for the existence of a style or language specific to any given work. This style should be such that Buffon's statement, "Le style, c'est l'homme" might better read, "le style, c'est le texte."[30] Since any text, therefore, can be said to have a style that is idiosyncratic to varying degrees, then surely this style is already inscribed by a virtual multitude of formal repetitions even before the text suffers any particular reading. I say "virtual multitude" because, taking N. Ruwet's lead, we can assume that many iterative aspects of a text are not noticed by any one reader, or even group of readers, at a given moment, but that such aspects *may* be noticed at a later time. The search for these as yet un-systematized textual stimuli forms a large part of the present study.

*   *   *

Let us return now to Deleuze's formulation of the first type of repetition, and examine it in greater detail. We recall that his principal objection to the concept is that it takes models or originals for granted. In literary circles, the repercussions of this belief have been far-ranging. I shall cite two examples, the first concerning writing. Blinded by their assumption of an epistemological fixity of things, the great majority of critics were forced, until recently, to explain a text as the product of an unchanging source called the author. As Michel Foucault, among others, has attempted to demonstrate,[31] however, there are in reality far too many psychic, economic, and social variables working on and through an author for anyone to pinpoint such an imagined individual.

Moreover, because these unpredictable forces have existed throughout (literary) history, it is hardly astonishing that we must now modify this anachronistic term, author, with the aid of Jacques Lacan's *sujet clivé*, or with what Julia Kristéva calls *le sujet en procès*.[32] The concept thus introduced precludes any simplistic reduction of the speaking/writing subject to a single proper name, and transforms Descartes' self-evident "I" into a fundamentally more complex, dynamic entity: "Il ne s'agit pas de savoir si je parle de moi de façon conforme à ce que je suis, mais si quand j'en parle, je suis le *même* [emphasis mine] que celui dont je parle."[33]

This notion of a split subject, opposed as it is to a self-conscious, immobile author, will facilitate our comprehension of how several discrete textual features (repetitions) originate. Without it, such features would be hard to accept, even unimaginable, since they do not figure among the conventional aspects of a message. The message in question, of course, is that presumed, packaged content transmitted between two hypothesized, fixed poles (I/thou) during acts of spoken or written communication.[34] Even though most individuals do interpret writing in the same manner that they do speaking, the fact is that such a procedure will not always work very well. If it did, one could dispense with reading a book and simply ask someone else to read it to him aloud. This whole affair might be expressed in the following terms: "To say that all acts of speech are interpersonal relationships is not, as a proposition, the same as claiming that all interpersonal relationships are acts of speech."[35] In other words, listening and speaking do not equal reading and writing. The pair, hearing and saying, would be more closely analogous to the right side of this equation. Unlike the singular subject then, who engages in only a certain kind of communication, the concept of a divided self turns the literary text into a " . . . multiple source of *unpredictable* 'speech acts' whose real author remains undetermined . . ." (Eco, *Theory*, p. 276).

The second example—it, too, a weakness of this view of repetition— consists in compelling theorists to dismiss any slight modifications that derive from the actual process of copying anterior models as relatively unimportant to the ultimate "meaning" expressed by the literary work. In consequence, thinking they all know more or less what the poem under their particular brand of analysis is about, they understandably feel no real methodological obligation to zero in on the same textual copies of what they take to be a common signified. In the end, they unknowingly turn all these differences, or specific textual signs *they* observe, into so many versions of a supposed content pre-dating the text.[36] They never really ask whether there is any structural or functional difference between all iterative signals; that is, between those they choose and all other possibilities.

Here, Deleuze's second type of repetition, which he insists on calling *différence*, adds a completely new dimension to our discussion. If it is true, he argues, that "c'est toujours par rapport à une identité conçue, à une analogie jugée, à une opposition imaginée, à une similitude perçue que la différence devient l'objet de la représentation" (*DR*, p. 180), this does not necessarily mean that difference has to be thought of in this way. He is advocating that we at least try to understand it on its own terms as well, something we shall now try to accomplish by digressing to Jacques Derrida's pioneering work.

The term "difference" has intrigued modern literary critics ever since Derrida developed the closely related concept/neologism, *différance*.[37] Above all else, what *différance* introduced into literary circles was the supposition of a special supplement that graphism brings to the constitution of a sign. Whereas written words as we know them are supposed to replace human speech, this word somehow escaped or, at very least, undermined that symbolic process. In so doing, the "a" added something peculiar to it. This graphic addition made the new term irreducible to a single spoken word, since within the written form were contained the phonetic seeds for two separate types of differing: to *differ* from (in being), and to *defer* (in time). According to the classic view of writing, that was not supposed to happen. No gap or uncertainty is supposed to exist between the written and the spoken it replaces. By signaling this undecidability, therefore, Derrida succeeded in illustrating the specific otherness of writing.

On closer analysis, what Derrida challenges is the tradition that would have a written signifier represent some signified other than the signifier itself. He insists that every signifier is, and carries with it, a difference which in its turn only signifies other signifiers. It does not strictly stand for anything permanent because it exists solely in relation to other differences. In this light, our initial elaboration of the interpretive process, $T = T_1 + T_2 + T_3$, would already be misleading, since *to begin with* no text is simply itself. A more appropriate equation would take this shape: $T_1 + T_2 + T_3 = T_1' + T_2' + T_3'$, where (') marks the fundamental difference between an "opened" text,[38] and anything one could say about it.

The main thrust of Derrida's project is thus directed against the classic semiological model, according to which writing is distinguished from speaking "par l'épaisseur invisible, presque nulle, de telle *feuille* entre le signifiant et le signifié."[39] Objecting to Saussure's metaphor of a piece of paper, he claims that a text's unsaid meaning, its ultimate *signifié*, can never be decided or determined from the series of words on the page. As in dream-work, "le texte inconscient est déjà tissé de traces pures, de différences où s'unissent le sens et la force."[40] Such an underlying signified is nowhere present; it is instead ". . . constitué d'archives qui sont *toujours déjà des* transcriptions . . . toujours déjà, c'est-à-dire dépôts d'un sens qui n'a jamais été présent, dont le présent signifié est toujours reconstitivé à retardement . . . après coup, supplémentairement."[41]

As a result, the most readers can hope to interpret or draw conclusions about are the masks, disguises, vestiges, phantoms of an unknowable sender, and an unidentifiable message. The secondary or supplementary meaning drawn from these traces is the sole kind possible. Whenever a critic discovers such meanings in a poem, he is perforce relying on repetition in Deleuze's first sense. That is, he has made his way back to fixed topoi which he believes are repeated by certain syntagmatic and/or lexematic units within the text. Once again, these well-anchored places or *concepts* impose themselves in the reader's mind as what the poem is about, as the truths behind any assertion he might make about it.

Of course, knowing for sure whether those specific concepts were really present during the writing of the work is impossible, not to mention irrelevant. Here we are talking not only about the author's intention, but also about those other forces we alluded to in reference to Foucault's studies. Derrida's implication is that since we can never know enough about a society, an epoch, a writer, the language he used, or the literature he read, neither can we put our finger on any truth, or signified of the text. There is *no* signified, in the final analysis, that has not always already taken the shape of a necessarily unique signifier—necessarily, because every sign, by definition, has its own specific form, etymology, denotations, connotations, in a word, history.

Now if repetition in the first sense permits us to find truths in a given text, it is at the same time that which blinds us to any further insights into its poeticity. For it is what prevents us from becoming (other) along with the text we are analyzing. In short, repetition obliges us to take our fixed (individual or collective) knowledge of the poet's life, linguistic and literary heritage, and historical epoch as the measure of a text's past and potential features: "D'une part la répétition [d'un modèle antérieur] est ce sans quoi il n'y aurait pas de vérité: . . . d'un autre côté, la répétition est le mouvement même de la non-vérité: la présence de l'étant du texte s'y disperse, s'y multiplie par mimèmes, icônes, phantasmes, simulacres, etc."[42]

Using adjectives derived from Plato's own value judgments, Derrida qualifies these two movements as good and bad repetitions. The good type, analogous to Deleuze's second type of repetition, permits what Harold Bloom, quoting from Kierkegaard, calls a "recollecting forward."[43] This forward motion is born from the totally novel "meaning" or signified of living speech; the fleeting breath of life in the single moment it utters; that *present* model which has the potential to allow a return to or repetition of it. Nietzschean in spirit, its main function consists in instituting a model for a *future* repetition, or what Barthes called "le modèle d'un *devenir*."[44] Examples of these kinds of models form the basis of my third chapter.

The bad type, on the other hand, unfolds within the field of the already written, as does Deleuze's first king of repetition. It concerns a copy or token that harkens backwards to a well-anchored, *past* model, the always-already-present domain of signifiers. In both cases though, and in its very operation, repetition relies on that undefinable, unnameable difference which undermines the actual presence of what it is attempting to re-present. This irreducible difference, uniqueness or non-iterable *ontos,* intrinsic to both model and copy, is what sets in motion the copying process itself and, at the same time, condemns it to imperfection.

To clarify these theoretical points, let us examine the prose poem, "Le Pelèrinage de Sainte Anne."[45] It was written by Saint-Pol Roux, heralded by André Breton as one of the main precursors of Surrealism. It begins with a description of five young sailors whose physical attributes are compared to things of the earth. They are about to make an offering to Sainte Anne, the Godmother of Sailors ("La Marraine des Marins"): "Les cinq Gars de faïence, à la peau de falaise, aux yeux couleur d'océan qui s'apaise, vont, bras dessus, vers la chapelle peinte où, vieillement jolie, sourit la bonne Sainte." In exchange for their money, these "earthenware" boys hope to marry five young girls already promised to them. The girls are described in fragile and somewhat trifling terms, "les cinq Promises de procelaine mignonnes comme des joujoux." Now despite major differences in refinement, both earthenware and procelain derive from earth. They are also traditionally associated with a certain fragility, though porcelain is certainly much harder than earthenware. From this angle, these epithets can be said to copy a past model of fragility (in this case, a metaphor) which we commonly associate with young people—their too easily shattered dreams and ideals.

As the narrative continues, the boys realize they have forgotten to bring the planned offering to the saint from their home in the village. Suddenly, for reasons unclear to us, they get a notion to draw their knives, and begin to approach the sleeping girls. Kneeling in front of them, they undo the girls' clothes and cut out their hearts, hoping that these "cinq Coeurs battant de l'aile" will make a sufficiently worthy gift for the saint. After offering the hearts and going out of the church, the boys discover much to their chagrin that the girls have left them. It would seem that having lost their hearts, the girls are no longer capable of loving the boys who so impulsively ravished them. At this point, the narrator chooses to end his allegorical tale on the following sad note: "Tombent alors en *défaillance* [emphasis mine] les cinq Gars de faïence, tandis que disparaissent les cinq Promises de porcelaine emparfumeés de marjolaine."

From our perspective, what has happened stylistically is this: *faïence*, which initially repeated or copied a certain "pertinent characteristic" of a past linguistic model or seme (fragility) acts, in a second stage of our reading, as the *future* model for the textual copy, *défaillance*. That is to say, the morphophonemic supplement, or, if one prefers, formal singularity brought along by the first copy, *faïence, in its very copying* of the past model, fragility, causes two symbiotically related textual repetitions:

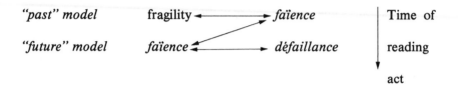

"past" model	fragility ⟷ *faïence*	Time of
"future" model	*faïence* ⟵ *défaillance*	reading
		act

Functioning as the denouement of the story, *défaillance* or "swooning" serves to underscore the narrative transition from the initial optimistic, joyful state of both the boys and girls to its eventual negation. The tale unfolds as if a would-be linguistic paradigm generated by *faïence* were then narratively "declined" to yield an apparent antonym, one beginning with the negative prefix, *dé-*. The earthenware boys are stripped of their essence, and become *non*-earthenware, so to speak.

Yet the irreducible difference of each element in this interconnected iterative series brings about an eventual occultation of the text's ultimate meaning. The occultation in question is provoked by the copying process itself. It forces us to wonder whether the poem is about the earth, earthenware, or swooning. Shifting back and forth among models and copies, the text's "meaning" no longer has any solid foundation or fixed place of privilege. The difference involved in repetition is, therefore, not (in a deconstructionist critic's words) ". . . what distinguishes one identity from another. It is not a difference between (or at least not between independent units), but a difference within these units. Far from constituting the text's unique identity, it is that which subverts the very idea of identity, indefinitely deferring the possibility of adding up the sum of a text's parts or meanings and reaching a totalized, integrated whole."[46]

Given this fact, however, one need not bother talking about some abstract, quasi-animate *différance,* but only about the two kinds of repetition it makes possible. For in pragmatic terms a specific linguistic model does serve in both cases as the point of departure for the perception, and most probably, production of style. What distinguishes between the two types is simply the spatio-temporal dimension of the reading act: where and when the model is located.

Although he still holds onto the word *différence* for the purposes of his study, it is clear then that for Deleuze, as well as for Derrida, the term really forms the other side of a coin called repetition. As Deleuze explains, one kind derives "du Même, qui s'explique par l'identité du concept ou de la représentation; la seconde est celle qui comprend la différence, et se comprend elle-même dans l'altérité de l'Idée, dans l'hétérogénéité d'une *apprésentation*" (*DR*, p. 36). For him also: "Les deux répétitions ne sont pas indépendantes. L'une est le sujet singulier, le coeur et l'intériorité de l'autre, la profondeur de l'autre. L'autre est seulement l'enveloppe extérieure, l'effet abstrait . . . c'est le masque, le déguisé, le travesti qui se trouve être la vérité du nu" (*DR*, p. 37).

If difference be that movement indispensable to all creation ("les masques"), and especially to literary creation, it is because without it nothing could ever have come to be, except perhaps Being itself. Without it, all literature might have stayed in the form of one book, a book that would have occasioned no new versions, translations, commentary, or other stories. As in Mallarmé's view ("le monde est fait pour aboutir à un beau livre"), it would have summarized the collective poetic experience of the entire world, and would have rendered the whole idea of a "new" work unthinkable. Mallarmé's preoccupation with this notion may explain in part why his work has been central to the style and theory of those critics most concerned with difference: Derrida, Lacan, and Kristéva. Whatever the case, the fact remains that difference can never be fully articulated, since difference is precisely that which permits the functioning of language itself. The closest one can come to this articulation is past and future repetitions.

As seductive as this two-stage theory of repetition may be, the latter's reputation is bound to cause a certain critical resistance to it. But in defense of our theory, Charles Mauron, for one, believes that because creation *ex nihilo* is inconceivable, "elle implique un néant préalable, lui-même précédé (si le mot n'avait déjà perdu tout son sens) par un Etre absolu."[47] Rephrasing this in the light of our previous observations vis-à-vis common interpretative practice: when a critic notices what he construes to be a significant stylistic aspect of a text, he immediately begins to seek out models which would explain its linguistic derivation. Though he assumes that any one model was a copy at some earlier time, he eventually ends his search and decides upon The Model.[48]

Yet Derrida rejects any "Etre absolu" or transcendental origin whatsoever. In effect, he replaces this originary model with an infinite regress of signifiers, itself a kind of origin. The upshot is that any time a signifier's signified cannot be satisfactorily decided upon, this act of deconstruction ends. It ends and necessarily falls short of its stated goal. For while it must be taken as referential to make certain points, "the deconstruction has been undertaken in order to deny the referentiality of the language in question!"[49]

In this sense, Derrida's grammatology fails to escape the same notion of symbolic repetition that it aspires to deconstruct. By repeating the language of the model *from which (à partir de)* it starts writing, this "science" calls attention to its own provisional, undecidable essence *qua* signifier and tries to pass itself off as the exemplary written text. In the meantime, what has continued to elude it is the difference it tries so desperately to evoke. At most, Derrida's enterprise amounts to a "contemplation à la dérive," stuck in a "redondance sans renouveau, non-productive . . . simplement variante précieuse à l'intérieur de l'enclos symbolique."[50] What his writing can never accomplish is to say that which has never been written before: the being (*ontos*) of a subject (or object, a text), and the conditions for his/its speech (*parole*) in the moment of his/its enunciation.[51] While trying to write "it" (difference), this originary writing or *archi-écriture* is forced to utilize a language that repeats what has already been said before about someone or something else, and which ineluctably means something else.

Given the essentially self-defeating nature of his analysis then, how can Derrida presume to call grammatology a "positive science?" How can writing the trace of a trace, the copy of a copy, ever amount to anything more than an erudite, highly sophisticated etymology? Before answering, Derrida recalls that, though doomed in language, the search for difference does not lead to a nostalgic longing for a final name or term. Not even the word *différance* suffices. It is no doubt significant that right after he talks about this nostalgia, which he does by using a negation: "il n'y aura pas de nom unique, fût-il le nom de l'être. Et il faut le penser sans nostalgie,"[52] his article ends. Freud, we remember, pointed to the mind's astuteness in divulging certain repressed wishes and desires by first negating them.[53] Is Derrida exposing his own nostalgia for something whose mention leaves him literally speechless?

In any event, the real purpose of his quest, he continues, is a Nietzschean affirmation of the elusiveness of *différance* through the writing process itself, or what he calls "*un certain rire, un certain pas de danse.*"[54] As provocative as these images are, they unfortunately smack of the kind of impressionistic vagueness we find in the *je ne sais quoi* of early stylistics and aesthetics. One might ask, for instance, exactly how writing laughs or dances. To adopt this perspective on the critic's role is furthermore to run the risk of being laughed at in one's turn, since it changes texts from fixed moments of inscribed History into points of departure for one's own playful (*ludique*) activity. It also risks devalorizing literature by raising commentary up to the same level. Because of this critical stance, Derrida will therefore reject the specificity of literary texts. And that, in the final analysis, is one of his most revolutionary ideas, especially as they pertain to the domain of literary criticism.

There are two drawbacks to his view that I feel need to be mentioned here. In the first place, the language of literature seems to me to be capable of signifying more, i.e., functioning more semiotically, than any other usage of a language. The issue of meaning's undecidability, as I intend to demonstrate, is exacerbated in artistic works. Moreover, I would suggest that a literary text's language functions, or malfunctions, differently from that of other writing. By underlining parameters like the reader or the context, one need not hypothesize a distinct poetic language in order to show this.

Derrida's inquiry into the *devenir-littéraire du littéral*[55] is nevertheless a pressing matter. While in non-literary usage signifiers evoke real things in the world (referents) for the people who read them, this is not always true for the literary text. Oftentimes, for example, a word in a poem functions primarily with respect to a word in another poem, as an allusion, and not to some material object. For this reason, the student of poetics should go back to the root of his problem, i.e., the signifiers whose signifieds cause so much disagreement among critics, and only later try to ascertain whether they are somehow different from those in "ordinary" texts; and, if so, how. To put all this in other terms, before reaching the hazier, less agreed-upon level of the signified—something one always does eventually—the reader must give a better account of what the poem actually gives him in the perceptible form of graphemes and their corresponding phonemes. That is the logical point of departure for a study of literariness, of how the literal becomes literary.

From here on, therefore, our approach will be explicitly structuralist; that is, provided Jameson is correct when he asserts that "the most characteristic feature of Structuralism lies precisely in a kind of transformation of form into content."[56] We are temporarily putting aside the question, "What is a poem about?", in order to attack the more fruitful question, "How does the poem manifest (it)?" If we never got back to the former, we would obviously produce nothing more than a linguistic analysis of the grammar of a text. On the other hand, how can we know what a work is about until we have seen the way "it" is expressed? The object thus placed between parentheses and quotation marks becomes of secondary interest. Like those absences in Japanese culture, which Barthes tells us define the center of their cities, gifts, rooms, gestures,[57] the "meanings" of our prose poems will be subordinated to their respective envelopes, their forms.

This comparison unfortunately leaves some trace of a center or referent in our conceptualization of poeticity. While letting the idea of an *outside* slip in almost imperceptibly, it reinvokes the traditional view that literature, through rhetorical stylization, adorns and embellishes a specific, reducible content. What my particular analysis attempts to treat is mainly these ornaments, these visual and acoustic stimuli. Indeed, it envisages anything other than them as interesting material at best, arbitrary and dangerous at worst.

The temptation to guess the point or purpose of a given text will likely always exist, however. Ultimately, we cannot do very much to counteract it; nor should we, necessarily. Though I risk being labelled an apologist for a more traditional, anti-scientific approach to literature in making this last statement, I must confess that one of my great reading pleasures consists in trying to guess as many of these points as possible. I suspect that I am not alone in this enterprise. Nevertheless, I would submit that description must not only precede, but also *predominate* in any interpretation, such that the latter remains primarily an extra-textual activity. Being extra-textual, it can be justified only marginally by the letter of the text. More generally, it is determined by the reader's own subjectivity, sex, historical situation, and adherence to a given socio-economic class.

As a result, this tendency to rationalize makes it essential to enumerate features that everyone can accept without much hesitation. This new obligation forces us once again to place our faith in the one area on which all literature depends, its graphemes and phonemes. So whatever lies outside of this reservoir, like Reality, for instance, will have to be bracketed in doubt, since there never has been, nor can there ever be very much agreement on it.

Now although some notion of a referent is a necessary condition to the design of my or any interpretive system—a notion, without which, one could not understand the present series of black spots—it is not a necessary condition for its *semiotic functioning* (Eco, *Theory*, p. 58). What this means is that literature's comprehensibility is not situated in those innumerable referents which pass through the reader's mind while he reads, but rather in the manner these referents present themselves. In other words, "l'intelligibilité ne serait pas d'abord dans la réalité (dont la diversité des descriptions montre toute la mouvance), mais dans l'articulation, dans la construction systématique et contraignante qui en est donnée et qui s'exprime au niveau du discours."[58]

This essentially linguistic construction, symbolic articulation, or "classe de variables," as Courtès calls it, I shall call *form*. As Valéry indicates, although not exactly in the same vein," la forme est essentiellement liée à la répétition."[59] Having already analyzed this phenomenon in some detail, we know that there are in fact two sides to its operation. It is not as simple as we used to think. We have seen that the functioning of a repetition depends, both at the start and at the finish, on an assumed, stable model. For it to happen at all it has to replicate something which necessarily comes from the past. At the same time, however, and in this very process of replicating, some sort of difference is created that brings with it the possibility of its future repetition.

If I may be permitted a final digression, the structure of families offers an interesting analogy that sheds some light on this point. A child "repeats" his parents corporally through his genes, and symbolically through his father's name (*Nom-du-Père*). Simultaneous to that, he adds the distinctiveness of his own body. Later in life, the child's body will have the potential to give rise to another child who, in turn, will repeat, etc., etc.[60] Although her intention was quite different from mine, Kristéva said something analogous when she wrote, "Ainsi, pourrions-nous dire qu'on répète la mère, mais qu'on imite le père . . . "[61] Her choice of "imitates" instead of "repeats" results more from her concern for (sexual) difference than from her description of how repetition works. Even so, to pursue the comparison between her point of view and mine, let us see the mother as a metaphor for the model, and the father as the force behind the replication. Their "child," the textual repetition, is born of the mother, literally, the *matrix* (the *semiotic*), and becomes otherwise named, identified, and recognized thanks to the father (the *symbolic*). This movement from mother to father was what Derrida referred to as repetition's vacillation between the realms of semiotic Non-truth and a symbolic Truth.[62] It explains why we *say* (that is, fall back into "le symbolique") that a structure exists in a poem. We say, or otherwise symbolically articulate it because, if no one else did either, the structure would, literally, not be "said" to exist. Instead, it would remain in that Platonic *chora* defined by Kristéva as: "une totalité non-expressive constituée par ces pulsions [infantiles, pré-symboliques] et leur *stases* en une motilité aussi mouvementée que réglementée."[63]

Now that we conceive of repetition "differently," our attitudes about both writing, and those structural features of literariness mentioned earlier—parallelisms, equivalences, and the rest—must change. A classificatory system can be imagined that would summarize all formal aspects of poeticity into two major types, corresponding to repetition's inherent dualism. The first would cover those parts of a text which re-present various things from outside its own margins. The second would include everything that acts as a model for another repetition within the text. This opposition has the advantage of amalgamating most critical approaches to literature into a simpler scheme through its emphasis of the criterion that theorists rely on to do their analyses: the repetition of various traits.

Before advancing, I shall designate the two types of repetition *intertextual* and *intratextual*. Since these terms have been used in countless other contexts it would be wise to explain what I mean by them in greater detail. The former comprises all aspects of a poem the perception of which presupposes a certain lingustic *and* literary[64] competence on the part of the reader. Anyone who speaks, writes, and reads a language has some degree of both competences in it. The combination of the two produces his language memory. By virtue of living within a society that utilizes a given language, this multi-talented person serves as a vehicle through which pass several of its discourses, "literary" and "non-literary" texts, clichés, stereotypes, descriptive systems, adages, proverbs, as well as much of its art, music, ideology, and history. Exposed to these and many other Culture "units" over a long period, he ends up storing this information, more or less completely, as would some unverifiable computer. If he somehow managed to retain nothing at all of his culture, he could neither talk, nor write, nor read, nor understand, nor communicate in any way with his compatriots.

What this retention represents to the individual, therefore, is Reality itself, or that which seems to exist outside of him, in spite of him. Whenever he perceives something in the world, a text, for example, he intermittently remembers certain material retained from his "sociolect." Ostensibly unable to stop himself, he becomes aware of, and often articulates, such reminiscences about which we infer the following: that on some level of his psyche, the person has judged, decided, chosen, determined that the present object repeats a (past) model. If a reader gets the uncanny feeling[65] that something he is reading exists or existed somewhere outside or before the text in which he finds it, we surmise that he has discovered an intertextual repetition.

Given the incalculable diversity of a sociolect, no one could presume to see all possible intertextuality. The farthest criticism can go in this domain is to gather the greatest number of reactions to a text that it can. By cataloging what a poem reminds many readers of, one obtains a sum of readings which approaches an all-inclusive intertextual reading. In the end, this projected reading would have little to do with any specific readers, since it is really more a question of people's (re)actions than of people themselves. In all probability, the confusion over what was coined Super-reader (*archi-lecteur*) could thus have been avoided if the term had been Super-reading (*archi-lecture*).[66]

The reactions this overall reading comprehends are next checked for accuracy by reference to the established, immobile models or topoi of a given society: dictionary definitions, linguistic norms, native speaker responses, and literary examples. When a particular word, phrase, or genre can be traced back in this fashion to a previous one, most critics will agree that a potential poetic feature is there.[67] Yet the more these intertextual repetitions mount up, the more they start reminding readers of certain models which these same readers cannot always convince others are really being copied. Slowly but surely, these readers get trapped in a vast network of cross-references between extra-textual models that turns their attention away from the text in hand to all those *others* it repeats. When I say "others," I am suggesting that an individual not only can, but does recall many referents during his analysis of a poem that are not strictly language-based: biographical and psychological details about the author, economic and historical factors, and the like. When this occurs en masse, as it did especially in the days of impressionistic criticism à la Thibaudet, the more scientifically oriented members of literary circles apparently fight back to restore the primacy of the text under scrutiny.

Anyone aware of modern thought in such circles recognizes in this last sentence the cause for so-called New Criticism, a movement decidedly too polyvalent for us to define any more. Nevertheless, as is well known, this movement's biggest achievement was to emphasize the peculiar form and internal structure of literature. Indeed, *intra*textual repetitions (or repetitions of unities that are not immediately, though eventually identifiable with intertextual models) now represent the second half, as it were, of textuality, as well as a major source and/or target of much contemporary literary commentary. That a text contains several types of models whose intra-textual repetition produces various formal aspects of its poeticity is currently a truism. But classical rhetoricians already knew that, and had invented terms like anaphora, accumulatio, repetitio, and many others long before structuralists began searching for finer, less evident repetitive features of literariness. I need not bother, therefore, insisting any longer on their significance.

Intertextual repetitions occur then when an external or past model is re-presented by what one judges to be a copy in the text one is reading. The intratextual variety has a model one first perceives *within* the present text's margins. The latter can be thought of as a "future" repetition inasmuch as what was construed to be The Model in the initial connection between the present text's linguistic units reveals itself *afterwards* to be also a less evident copy of something familiar from before. Thus, an intratextual model is the sign of an as yet undiscovered intertextual model. We can summarize the two iterative processes in this fashion:

Intertextual — *past* model first recognized by a given reader in a *present* textual copy, later seen by the same reader to be copied by other elements of the *present* text.

Intratextual — *present* model, first identified through copies of the *present* text, later recognized ("future") as a less evident copy of a *past* model.[68]

Because the literary and linguistic competence brought to a text varies from reader to reader, any particular poetic feature may thus strike one individual as having its most immediate linguistic origin (model) within the present text. But another reader, who is better versed in literature and/or the grammar of his own language, may very well see the same feature as an obvious copy of something from a different text, without any special reference (at first) to the present context. In both cases, however, the special category of readers known as literary critics will sooner or later have to get back to commonly shared beliefs, myths, and stereotypes in order that their interpretations mean something to other people.

It is significant that Saussure, too distinguishes between linguistic elements *in praesentia* and *in absentia*, although he makes this distinction in reference to all language, not just literature. However, when Jakobson integrates these paradigmatic and syntagmatic axes into his classic formulation of the "poetic function," a subtle twist is brought into the notion of past and present dimensions of a text, or what I call its outside and inside. The twist is this: through the "natural" process alluded to earlier, absent aspects of a text are immediately construed to be the referents, and are treated like semantic elements. The present aspects are embodied by the text's form. In one of the more powerful and convincing avatars of Jakobson's notion, structural stylistics, texts are thus seen to engender, and be engendered by two different relationships, semantic and formal.[69]

It has also come to be said that poetic discourse is the equivalence "between a word and a text, or a text and another text."[70] Yet seeing how the semantic side of a text is ultimately undecidable, it is impossible for us anymore not to devalorize it in proportion to its strictly formal side. Rather than dismiss *a priori* anything other than texts, phrases, and words as irrelevant to the private domain of poeticity, Jakobson maintains that "tout élément linguistique s'y trouve converti en figure du langage poétique."[71] This suggests that every linguistic element in an artistic work—syllables, letters, accents—has the power to add something meaningful to the whole, provided we take it seriously.

This is an important qualification. For if we took such elements seriously in "non-artistic" works, we have no reason to believe that they, too, would not add something meaningful to the whole utterance. Our assumption therefore—a corollary to Jakobson's poetic theory—is that a literary work tends to force the reader into taking the linguistic forms on the page more seriously than a non-literary one. Of course, since the grosser linguistic models (words, texts) resemble aspects of "ordinary" communication, they tempt the reader to search for meaning more than those other elements do. In so doing, they divert his eyes from other, less recognized formal features which may, in fact, help him distill the particularity of literature.

For these reasons it is necessary to place less stock at first in semantic components than in phonemes and graphemes. Instead of looking at texts exclusively for something conforming to the *consensus omnium* (which only tells us what we already know), we stand to gain much from analyzing them first and foremost as the pieces of paper they are. The signifying markers (signifiers) on these papers are, after all, what we, as users of a given language, perceive and then interpret. This does not mean that written words do not have specific denotations and connotations, verifiable by their other occurrences in the language. But whenever something in the text reminds us of such external models, let us simply place it under the intertextual rubric of our typology, and not fall prey to any transcendental, absolute meaning it may appear to possess. Before deciding how a given piece of writing comes to be labeled as "literature," therefore, we would be well advised to read it first as words, words, words. That, I think, is the sense of Mallarmé's comment to Degas, when he claimed he wrote poetry with words, not ideas.

* * *

Having explained how repetition works, I can now undertake an actual analysis of what is repeated. My choice of a first text would ideally center on a group of words that has been designated as "literary," but which, superficially, does not present itself as such. That is, it would have no conventional aspects, like accent, meter, rhyme, paragraph or chapter sections, to tip off the reader as to its artistic lineage.[72] The less clear-cut meaning it had, the more it would suit our testing purposes. In short, the ideal starting point for our study of iteration in literature would be a text whose signifiers acted more like pure forms than as the backsides of signifieds. *Poisson soluble* no. 11 is just such a text:

> La place du Porte-Manteau, toutes fenêtres ouvertes ce matin, est sillonée par les taxis à drapeau vert et les voitures de maîtres. De belles inscriptions en lettres d'argent répandent à tous les étages les noms des banquiers, des coureurs célèbres. Au centre de la place, le Porte-Manteau lui-même, un rouleau de papier à la main, semble indiquer à son cheval la route où jadis ont foncé les oiseaux de paradis apparus un soir sur Paris. Le cheval, dont la crinière blanche traîne à terre, se cabre avec toute la majesté désirable et dans son ombre ricochent les petites

lumières tournantes en dépit du grand jour. Des fûts sont éventrés sur le côté gauche de la place; les ramures des arbres y plongent par instants pour se redresser ensuite couvertes de bourgeons de cristal et de guêpes démesurément longues. Les fenêtres de la place ressemblent à des rondelles de citron, tant par leur forme circulaire, dite oeil de boeuf, que par leurs perpétuelles vaporisations de femmes en déshabillé. L'une d'elles se penche sur la visibilité des coquilles inférieures, les ruines d'un escalier qui s'enfonce dans le sol, l'escalier qu'a pris un jour le miracle. Elle palpe longuement les parois des rêves, comme une gerbe de feu d'artifice qui s'élève au-dessus d'un jardin. Dans une vitrine, la coque d'un superbe paquebot blanc, dont l'avant, gravement endommagé, est en proie à des fourmis d'une espèce inconnue. Tous les hommes sont en noir mais ils portent l'uniforme des garçons de recette, à cette différence près que la serviette à chaîne traditionnelle est remplacée par un écran ou par un miroir noir. Sur la place du Porte-Manteau ont lieu des viols et la disparition s'y est fait construire une guérite à claire voie pour l'été.

The text begins with a description of La place du Porte-Manteau as it might appear during a special celebration. In the center of the square we find the Porte-Manteau himself, along with his horse, some wine casks, and trees covered with crystal and unusually long wasps. Breton has played with the name of the square and personified it into the primary denotation of the signifier *porte-manteau,* an officer who carries the cloak of an important personage. The description now begins to remind me of other surrealist texts where equally fantastic happenings are encountered. On this gross level then, a first intertextual repetition has already occurred. I am alerted to the fact that I can no longer read the text as I would a bit of realistic prose (even though, frankly, I am not so certain what "realistic" means any more).

In any case, these details are now comprehensible only insofar as they repeat a form of description I, and probably others, think we have seen before. All of a sudden, something happens that seems totally different. Remembering that difference can only be conceived of as the other side of repetition, I decide to focus in on this different, or "new" feature. I start seeking out the intertextual model it is repeating or, if that option fails, the intratextual model it institutes. The feature assumes the form of a comparison whose soundness is problematic: "Les fenêtres de la place ressemblent à des rondelles de citron, tant par leur forme circulaire, dite oeil

de boeuf, que par leurs perpétuelles vaporisations de femmes en déshabillé."
Thanks to another intertextual model (the standard syntactical form of a
comparison: A resembles B because of C and D), I can assume that at least
some aspects of these windows are repeated *intra*textually by the term
rondelles de citron. This syntactical form leads me to believe that two of the
windows' aspects are also repeated by the words *forme circulaire* and
perpétuelles vaporisations.

Beyond that, my reading falters. Whereas the former syntagm, *forme
circulaire,* repeats the socially recognized seme "roundness" intrinsic to a
round lemon slice, the latter, *perpétuelles vaporisations,* repeats nothing at
all readily reminiscent of something else. The first reaction of most readers
would be to rationalize this semantic difficulty as just one more intertextual
feature of so-called automatic writing. Like other automatic works, they
reason, this one too contains various semantic anomalies endemic to the
genre. Assuming that our views on the repetitive process are correct, there
should nevertheless be an element within the words *perpétuelles vaporisations*
(an element consequently *intra*textual) which makes of them a legitimate
copy of the intertextual comparison model. Failing to locate this element is
tantamount to ignoring the fact that a (past) syntactic structure forces the
present collocation of graphemes to take the shape of a socially recognized
comparison. So the reader's task is to determine how this text in particular
accomplishes that feat. To describe its literary functioning, he has to find
some feature within the poem's margins which formally actualizes that
cultural model.

The text has thereby cheated us in a sense. For a short time it acted
like something we all "knew," but then abruptly changed its narrative
course, leaving most of us in the dark. The only solution to such scriptural
treachery is to stop thinking in intertextual terms of dictionary meaning
alone, and to start looking more carefully at the forms which caused the
problem in the first place.

This procedure of retroactive reading gives us instant results. The
semantic incompatibility[73] we observed between the two vehicles of the
tenor *rondelles* is quickly resolved by the latter's mere graphemic nature.
For if one were to cut this word into two syllables, *rond* and *elles*, both
halves would develop narratively without a hitch. The first is generated in
relation to an outside model or *inter*textually; the second, in relation to a
text-based model or *intra*textually. That the idea of dividing occurred to
Breton in writing this story should not surprise anyone, since intertextually,
"folding" or "dividing" constitutes a connotation of the word *porte-
manteau,* and *a fortiori,* the word *rondelles.* Without the concept of a split
(!) subject, it would be hard to believe that he meant to write such an image.
Few writers realize that much about what they are trying to say.

Just the same, some authors might at least concede that that is in fact what they *are* saying through their writing, even if they accept their having expressed such things in spite of themselves. Here, the text itself suggests that these two parts exist separately. It expresses this division syntactically by the pattern *tant par . . . que par . . . .* The first part of *rondelles* by itself forms an adequate model permitting the text to produce the copy *forme circulaire.* On the denotative level—by definition, intertextual—it does not need the part *elles* in order to remind us of roundness. The simple form or morpheme *rond* suffices. Moreover, this intratextual copy *forme circulaire* becomes the model for still another copy inside this text. Our linguistic competence from before or outside of this text tells us that an *oeil de boeuf* is a kind of window with a circular form. Thus, the conventional form of a comparison expands the first syllable in a more or less typical manner. A modicum of cognitive effort is required to follow the progression: windows➤ round➤ circular➤ *oeil de boeuf.*

The second part, however, serves as a much less familiar model. Whereas *rond* evokes a sufficiently large semantic field for most people to understand the above expansion, the *elles* is confusing. Seeing its pronominal form, it is impossible to know what it replaces, or even whether it replaces anything. If I put aside the signified for a moment and concentrate on the signifier, I discover a grapho-phonemic repetition close by in *perpétuelles.* Normally following a noun, this adjective can, like many others we recall, be placed before it for certain stylistic reasons. To quote Grevisse, "la combinaison *adjectif + nom* est très fortement sentie comme une unité de pensée: il y a alors un seul accent d'intensité." In this context, *perpétuelles* precedes the group *vaporisations de femmes en déshabillé,* making its "meaning" more tightly attached, so to speak, to the corresponding nominal syntagm. These two observations, combined with the start of the very next sentence, "L'une d'*elles* [emphasis mine]," imply that the form *elles* is being intratextually developed to signify something. The writing, if not the writer as well, seems to want to have me read the second part of *rondelles* as thoroughly as I did the first.

Since I know I am reading literature, this intratextual repetition of *elles* impels me to identify something outside of the text which is repeated from within by this grapho-phonemic cluster. If *rond* generated the idea of circularity, I retrospectively deduce that from its first appearance *elles,* too, had a similar potential to conjure up a sociolectic unit. This unit corresponds to a third person feminine pronoun that signifies "them" (women). The next sentence, indeed, produces the copy, *femmes.* Once this extended female presence has been established on the level of the writing, the narrator begins talking about a specific woman. *L'une d'elles,* as if her existence and location were perfectly well known. But is she real or a vaporization? Why does she suddenly become important to the narration? The apparent result of a simple graphemic repetition *(elles),* how does she attract the writer's attention and make her way into the story? As her relationship to the rest of the narrative will soon be explained, I shall suspend this inquiry here.

In the meantime, I can schematize the extended metaphor between windows and lemon slices:

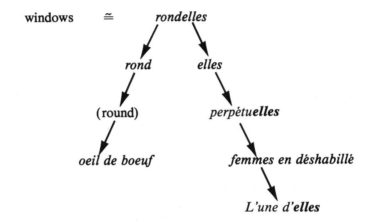

By noting the repetition of mere forms, I arrive at a textual logic that can be summed up like this: windows are related to lemon slices as much by a steer's eye as by an unclad woman. Although these last two elements are not necessarily connected, the text will progressively justify their seemingly gratuitous juxtapositon. The precise manner in which it accomplishes this remains to be seen.

What I know at present is that, had I not taken the time to consider these forms, I would have been at a real loss when reading the rest of the text. For the initial characters we met all disappeared. A scantily clothed woman, ("*L'une d'elles*"), a superb ocean liner, and men dressed in black take their places in the story. So either the narrative sequence has been disrupted once again—and this time, one may fear, for good—or else, the text will somehow reconnect the otherwise broken narrative pieces.

Returning to the source of this new incongruity, I reread the sentence which describes the woman leaning out of her window: "L'une d'elles se penche sur la visibilité des coquilles inférieures, les ruines d'un escalier qui s'enfonce dans le sol, l'escalier qu'a pris un jour le miracle." Given her state of undress, I suddenly recall other scenes from our collective mythology (bar rooms, red light districts), where such a gesture is associated with a certain eroticism, sometimes even licentiousness. Bending over into a field of vision exposes the partially dressed female to inquisitive, roving eyes, which can be dangerous. This past memory next leads me back to the text, and makes me wonder about the *oeil de boeuf* in the preceding sentence. Is this term to be taken literally, as was *portemanteau*? Does this steer's eye metonymically replace or repeat the eye of a sexually aroused man staring at this unsuspecting lady? Let us continue our reading for answers.

The *coquilles* over which she is bending seem just as gratuitous as did the word *rondelles*. Why shells? Since all copies are supposed to act as models in their turn, is it possible that the graphemic similarity[74] between the two terms gives rise to some small part of this text's literariness? Let us see what happens when we divide this new word: *coqu - illes*. Based on the model of *rond*, the first half comes very close (graphemically) to the signifier for rooster (*coq*).[75] Is this word fragment repeating the intertextual codes (animal and human, respectively) attached to a steer and an attractive woman, as in the cliché, *le coq du village* (the most attractive man)? Is the second part, *illes*, a kind of graphic reminder or copy of the form *elles* which, in contrast to the feminine form, hints at the idea of men? The text alone can confirm these speculations.

The necessary rapprochement of *rondelles* and *coquilles*, two signifiers that produce extraordinary images, is nevertheless increasingly corroborated for the reader by the writing itself. Earlier we observed the first of these words split in half and develop in two different directions. If the poetic function truly relates these two words formally, then our analysis of repetitive aspects must reveal a similar expansion of *coquilles*.

While anxiously waiting to see whether the poem produces this additional poetic feature, we learn more about the woman. It is said that she "palpe longuement les parois des rêves, comme une gerbe de feu d'artifice qui s'élève au-dessus d'un jardin." As with the syntactical pattern in the comparison to lemon slices, this phrase's structure (*palper les parois de* _____) prepares us for any number of stereotypical objects that our linguistic competence would help provide. "Palpating a wall of _____ " usually refers to a part of the human body; the stomach wall, for example. But what this woman turns out to be feeling is, in fact, *im*palpable, i.e., dreams. If we consider that the woman is bending over, semi-clothed, dreaming, gazing out her window, and feeling walls, it is not too outrageous to correct this lexical "mistake" (or to borrow a term from classical rhetoric, *catachresis),* in the following way. The walls she is "really" touching are those of her vagina. Although the word does not actually figure on the page, it is retrieved from our sociolect because of the intertextual repetition of a related pattern in its environment. To be sure, my knowledge of the rest of the story renders this explanation more probable than it is on the first reading. Anyone who analyzes a poem, though, has presumably read it completely.

This external reference (vagina) immediately draws my attention to another part of the poem itself, the word *gerbe*. In a flash, this word throws me back outward to the often quoted line from Victor Hugo's poem "Booz Endormi": "Sa gerbe n'était point avare ni haineuse." I am reminded that Hugo's poem, in an equally discrete manner, presents sexual imagery, but makes explicit only Boas's dream and Ruth's desire. The relevance of this intertextual recollection is affirmed in the very next line of Breton's text. There we are introduced to a new "character," one whose affiliation with the narrative is stressed by what its written form repeats: "Dans une vitrine, la *coque* [emphasis] d'un superbe paquebot blanc, dont l'avant, gravement endommagé, est en proie à des fourmis d'une espèce inconnue." The supplementary poetic feature we thought might spring forth out of *coquilles* finds its echo or copy (*coque*) establishes a formal equivalence among the objects in close proximity to the unclad woman, the shells and the ship. Thanks to this, the reader begins to discern a developing, possibly erotic, adventure between them.

At the same time, an interesting conversion occurs. Whereas the cluster *elles* is repeated intratextually, *illes* generates intertextual copies, *un superbe paquebot blanc* and *tous les hommes sont en noir*. What is repeated here is not the graphemic shape of *illes,* but rather its approximate meaning as a third person masculine pronoun, "the men." At first, *elles* signified vaporizations of semi-clothed wom*en,* and only afterward switched to one particular wom*an*. The expansion of *illes,* however, works in the reverse order: *a* superb, white oceanliner becomes *the* men in black.

It may be objected that an oceanliner is in fact not a man. Although that can certainly be conceded outside of our text, the repetition of *coqu* within it sets up an *ad hoc* identity between them. The only part of the ship described, its *coque,* metonymically replaces the whole *paquebot,* and carries along with it extra sexual connotations that have already been intertextually inferred. Owing to his perception of these repetitions, the retroactive reader realizes, moreover, that this image of an attractive woman activates the idiolectic counterpart, *superbe paquebot blanc,* of a cliché. The cliché I have in mind is that of a tall, handsome man. Being white, this man/ship is set apart from the rest of the men, who are dressed in black. His sex-appeal and handsomeness derive from the word *superbe,* and are determined by the phonemic residue of the intratextual graphemic repetition, *coqu* ⟶ *coque* ⟶ *paque-bot* (read *beau*).

The last aberrant detail my reading focuses in on involves the common damage done to both the ship's prow, and the staircase leading up to the woman's apartment. The interpretation I give of it is based on the bulk of contextual clues this preliminary study of repetitions has provided. My general rule throughout this essay, in fact, is to evaluate any iterative features in strict accordance with the comprehensive signified or "thrust" I, like anyone else, am tempted to guess is operative in a given text. That one can guess at all, however, results from, and is the sign of, an anterior appraisal of certain repetitions. Such hermeneutic circularity is discussed at greater length in my final chapter.

This being stated, I recall that the front part of the ship/man suffers from a strange kind of ant infestation, "en proie à des fourmis d'une espèce inconnue." From an intertextual point of view, discomfort of this sort in a man repeats a cliché about having ants in one's pants. But in addition to that, ant infestation has a very specific scientific designation in French, namely, *formication*. Provided we are right in thinking this text is a disguised erotic scene (disguised until the end, that is), it is obvious why the author qualifies these ants as belonging to an "unknown species." He draws the reader's attention to them more effectively than he could by simply calling them ants. The reader wants to know what kind they "really" are.

And yet, in so doing, the author does not disclose the one word that would give away the whole unsaid "plot." The word, "for*n*ication," is paranomastically embedded within our intertextually derived scientific term, and differs from the latter by a tiny graphemic trait. Since, as we have seen, the woman's actions are seductive, she is thus obviously able to cause any male observer a certain amount of uneasiness, i.e. strange ants in his "hull." It is known that such malaise often results in a man's longing for, or impatient rush towards, the desired object. And if he is big enough, a man in this situation would hurt both himself and possibly even the staircase he took to reach the woman, just as the text says. In 1924, the year *Poisson soluble* was published, few objects were bigger than oceanliners.

The final sentence tells us that: "Sur la place du Porte-Manteau ont lieu des viols . . ." The attention we paid to all the formal repetitions saves us now from the perplexity this last incongruent detail would provoke in most other unsuspecting readers. Had we not trusted this "literary" text, and believed it capable of furnishing clues (intertextual and intratextual) for us to appreciate its peculiarity, we might still be trying to figure out what it means, instead of first learning how it means. Since figuring out a text's meaning(s) is tantamount to interpreting it, this critical gesture amounts to little more than indicating some of the many intertextual models a text may be shown to repeat. The critic who interprets Breton's poem thus has to point out exactly how it paints a scene of seduction, attempted rape, or some other comprehensible narrative situation before choosing one (or more) of these models over others. He is obliged to identify the different forms that this specific poem uses to manifest such stereotypical patterns.[76] For although patterns like the latter are always already articulated somewhere else, they can never re-present their *originality* except by assuming new formal configurations.

Seeing that only some of these forms were mentioned during this first analysis, establishment of even a preliminary iterative typology demands that many more of them be examined in the following chapters. As will be demonstrated, the two-stage repetition of forms allows readers to perceive and describe poeticity from the grossest level of the text (genre) to the finest level (accent marks and punctuation).[77] At this point, the one statement we can make with some assuredness is that the literary phenomenon seems to depend largely on the constant interaction, or zigzagging reading, of precise textual forms with never-present, phantom-like "meanings."

NOTES

[1]This implication becomes rather ironic when one understands that Malherbe himself did not avoid morphological, phonological, syntactic, and semantic repetitions in his own work. Nicolas Ruwet gives several good examples of such critical blindness on Malherbe's part in his "Malherbe: Hermogène ou Cratyle?" *Poétique*, 42 (1980), 195-224.

[2]See Henri Morier, *Dictionnaire de Poétique et Rhétorique* (Paris: Presses Universitaires de France, 1961), p. 346. Instead of a concise definition, we are referred to no fewer than nine other rhetorical figures which rely on repetition for their very functioning. There are many more.

[3]I therefore cannot agree with Paul B. Armstrong, who states in his article "The Conflict of Interpretation and Limits of Pluralism," *PMLA*, 98, No. 3 (May, 1983), 342: "Psychoanalysis, Marxism, Phenomenology, and Structuralism—each has a different set of convictions that make up its point of departure and define its position in the hermeneutic field." To say that these sciences all have a different metaphysics, a different set of convictions, and a different point of departure is not, after all, the same as saying that on the epistemological plane, they all proceed differently. Selecting different criteria does not imply that one necessarily does anything different with them. Indeed, on the same page, Professor Armstrong seems to support the very point I am trying to make here when he writes: "To embrace a type of interpretation is to make a leap of faith *by accepting one set of presuppositions* and rejecting others" (emphasis mine). In other words, the sets change; the act of accepting a set does not.

[4]Everyone's literary and linguistic competences are by definition limited, since he or she has not read every text ever written.

[5]This rehabilitation has already begun, though not exactly in the same manner I am describing here. In the past few years, several major literary critics have turned their attention to repetition. Among the most prominent are Jeffrey Mehlman, *Revolution and Repetition: Marx/Hugo/Balzac* (Berkeley: U. of Calif. Press, 1977); Joseph Hillis Miller, *Fiction and Repetition: Seven English Novels* (Cambridge: Harvard U. Press, 1982); Edward W. Said, *The World, The Text, and The Critic* (Cambridge: Harvard U. Press, 1983), especially his chapters entitled "On Repetition," pp. 111-125, and "On Originality," pp. 126-139; and virtually all of Jacques Derrida's work.

[6]Youri Lotman, *La Structure du texte artistique* (Paris: Gallimard, 1973), p. 286

[7]These terms are used in many contemporary critical works, but especially in those of Levin, Foucault, Riffaterre, Lacan, Derrida, Kristéva, Mauron, Jakobson, and Greimas. See my bibliography for exact references.

[8]Roman Jakobson most clearly developed these Russian Formalist notions in his *Essais de linguistique générale* (Paris: Editions de Minuit, 1963), pp. 209-38. Literariness is that phenomenon in which the poetic function ("the projection of the paradigmatic axis onto

the syntagmatic axis") predominates over any other communicational function of a language in a written text. It draws attention more to the form of an expression than to its content.

[9]Cf. Stanley Fish in "How Ordinary is Ordinary Language?", *New Literary History,* 5 (1973), 52: "Literature is still a category, but it is an open category, not definable by fictionality, or by a disregard of propositional truth, or by a statistical predominance of tropes and figures, but simply by what we decide to put into it. The difference [between literature and non-literature] lies not in the language, but in ourselves."

[10]Roland Barthes, *Le degré zéro de l'écriture* (Paris: Seuil, 1972).

[11]Lotman, *La Structure du texte artistique,* p. 165.

12Cf. Umberto Eco, *A Theory of Semiotics* (Bloomington & London: Indiana University Press, 1979). p. 97. (Hereafter cited as *Theory.*)

[13]Nicolas Ruwet, *Langage, Musique, Poésie* (Paris: Seuil, 1973), pp. 215-16.

[14]To mention some of the better known studies: Anna Balakian, *Literary Origins of Surrealism* (New York: King's Press, 1947); Suzanne Bernard, *Le poème en prose de Baudelaire jusqu'à nos jours* (Paris: Nizet, 1959); Maurice Nadeau, *History of Surrealism* (New York: Macmillan, 1965); and Marcel Raymond, *De Baudelaire au Surréalisme* (Paris: José Corti, 1952).

[15]The editions used herein are contained in Charles Baudelaire, *Oeuvres,* ed. Claude Pichois (Paris: Bibliothèque de la Pléiade, 1975), vol. 1: Arthur Rimbaud, *Oeuvres,* ed. Suzanne Bernard (Paris: Garnier, 1960); and André Breton, *Manifestes du Surréalisme* (Paris: Jean-Jacques Pauvert, 1962), respectively.

[16]I am aware that the question of any genre's specificity is actually an open one. Nevertheless, as I intend to show in this study, the prose poem could not function semiotically were it not for certain set notions of those formal features constitutive of other, more traditional genres. The second section of my last chapter deals more extensively with this problem, especially pp. 124-126.

[17]Michael Riffaterre, *Semiotics of Poetry* (Bloomington & London: Indiana University Press, 1978).

[18]Gilles Deleuze, *Différence et répétition* (Paris: PUF, 1972). (Hereafter cited as DR.)

[19]For a different, much less rigorous description of these two types of repetition, see Deleuze's *Logique du Sens* (Paris: Editions de Minuit, 1969), p. 302.

[20]This expression, as well as the belief in question, is used and criticized by Jacques Derrida throughout his *De la grammatologie* (Paris: Editions de Minuit, 1967).

[21]ed. Bernard, *Oeuvres,* p. 344.

[22]André Breton, *Nadja* (Paris: Gallimard, 1964).

[23]Charles Sanders Peirce's notion of an "interpretant" recalls this change of focus on the part of the observer. See his *Collected Papers* (Cambridge: Harvard University Press, 1931-1958), 1.339.

[24]Barthes explains that *naturalizing* is the most important function of myth. Following through with his argument, we might conclude that definitions themselves are the most pervasive, not to say insidious, myths of them all. See his *Mythologies* (Paris: Seuil, 1970), pp. 215-17.

[25]It goes without saying that the violence of this action is exacerbated when done to a human being, something which happens all the time. See Derrida, *De la grammatologie,* pp. 149-202.

[26]Norman Holland shares this same opinion of textual interpretation in his *5 Readers Reading* (New Haven & London: Yale University Press, 1975).

[27]For this whole issue of choosing see Jean-Joseph Goux, "Numismatiques," Partie I, *Tel Quel*, No. 35 (1968), 64-89.

[28]Cf. Gilles Deleuze, *Logique du sens,* p. 302: "Il s'agit de deux *lectures* [emphasis mine] du monde dans la mesure où l'une nous convie à penser la différence à partir d'une similitude ou d'une identité préalables, tandis que l'autre nous invite au contraire à penser la similitude et même l'identité comme le produit d'une disparité de fond. La première définit exactement le monde des copies ou des représentations; elle pose le monde comme icône. La seconde, contre la première, définit le monde des simulacres. Elle pose le monde lui-même comme fantasme."

[29]The expression is Nietzsche's, but Frederic Jameson adopts it as the title of his book, *The Prison-House of Language* (Princeton: Princeton University Press, 1972). Jameson alludes to the way, for Saussure, language, or more specifically, language's phonemes, signify only in relation to other phonemes. His intention is to suggest a possible alternative to that earlier linguistic theory, a new critical or "meta"-language.

[30]Quoted from Michael Riffaterre, *La Production du texte* (Paris: Seuil, 1979), p. 8.

[31]Michel Foucault, "Qu'est-ce qu'un auteur?", *Bulletin de la Société Française de Philosophie*, 63, No. 3 (1969), 73-104.

[32]Julia Kristéva, *Polylogue* (Paris: Seuil, 1977), pp. 55-106. Lacan's concept of a split subject, as distinct from that of a fixed subject, underlines the impossibility of situating the individual components in Freud's tri-partite psychic topology (ego, super-ego, id). Kristéva's coinage results from her incorporating the Lacanian term into her semiotic theory of art.

[33]Jacques Lacan, *Ecrits* (Paris: Seuil, 1966), p. 276.

[34]Emile Benveniste defends this point of view in his *Problèmes de linguistique générale* (Paris: Gallimard, 1966), pp. 225-50.

[35]Jameson, *The Prison-House of Language,* p. 205.

[36]This whole procedure is analyzed and criticized by Sylvère Lotringer in "Flagrant délire," *Semiotext(e) Saussure's Anagrams,* 2, No. 1 (1975), 90-112. His main target is the notion of a semantic matrix, as developed primarily by Riffaterre. In theory, this matrix is that absence or hole around which the whole text revolves. Deduced from words presented to the reader, it is the unsaid point or moral of the story.

[37]Jacques Derrida, "La Différance," *Théorie d'ensemble* (Paris: Seuil, 1968), pp. 41-66.

[38]The word is borrowed from Umberto Eco's *Opera aperta* (Milano: Bompiani, 1962). By "opened" I mean a text which is assumed to have more than one possible meaning, insofar as it provides a "multiple source of *unpredictable* 'speech acts' whose real author remains undetermined . . ."

[39]Jacques Derrida, *La Dissémination* (Paris: Seuil, 1972), p. 127.

[40]Jacques Derrida, *L'Ecriture et la différence* (Paris: Seuil, 1967), p. 314.

[41]Derrida, *L'Ecriture et la différence,* p. 314.

[42]Derrida, *La Dissémination,* p. 195.

[43]Harold Bloom, *The Anxiety of Influence: A Theory of Poetry* (New York: Oxford University Press, 1975), p. 83. This motion, reserved for whom Bloom calls the "strong poet," permits the poet to break forth into a "freshening that yet repeats his precursors' achievements."

[44]Roland Barthes, "Introduction à l'analyse structurale du récit," *Communications,* 8 (1966), 26-27. The preceding part of the phrase in which we find this expression reads: ". . . il se peut que les hommes réinjectent [my word, *repeat*] sans cesse dans le récit ce qu'ils ont connu, ce qu'ils ont vécu; du moins est-ce dans une forme qui, elle, a triomphé de la répétition et institue le modèle d'un devenir."

[45]Reproduced in Maurice Chapelan, *Anthologie du poème en prose* (Paris: René Juilliard, 1946), pp. 150-153. See my appendix for the entire text, pp. 136-137.

[46]Barbara Johnson, *The Critical Difference: Essays in the Contemporary Rhetoric of Reading* (Baltimore & London: Johns Hopkins University Press, 1980), p. 4.

[47]Charles Mauron, *Des Métaphores obsédantes au mythe personnel* (Paris: Corti, 1963), p. 233.

[48]It may well be that this decision is primarily made for the sake of some convenience. As such, it would entail distinctly ideological concerns. For more on this, see my pp. 120-121.

[49]J. Hillis Miller, "Deconstructing the Deconstructors," *Diacritics,* 5 (1975), 30.

[50]Julia Kristéva, *La Révolution du langage poétique* (Paris: Seuil, 1974), p. 133.

[51]Kristéva, *La Révolution du langage poétique,* p. 79.

[52]Derrida, "La Différance," p. 66.

[53]Sigmund Freud, "Negation," in *Standard Edition,* ed. James Strachey (London: Hogarth Press, 1953-74), 19, 235-39.

[54]Derrida, "La Différance," p.66.

[55]Derrida, *L'Ecriture et la différence,* p. 336.

[56]Jameson, *The Prison-House of Language,* p. 198.

[57]Roland Barthes, *L'Empire des signes* (Genève: Skira, 1970).

[58]Joseph Courtès, *Lévi-Strauss et les contraintes de la pensée mythique* (Paris: Monc, 1973), p. 176. For Courtès, as well as Greimas, meaning, signification, thruth, even reality itself, exist only insofar as they can be translated or *re-articulated* from one code to another, from one language to another.

[59]Paul Valéry, *Oeuvres,* ed. Jean Hytier (Paris: Bibliothèque de la Pléiade, 1957), II, 554. Since Valéry adds, "L'idole du nouveau est donc contraire au souci de la forme," it is clear that he is talking only about "past" repetitions.

[60]This operation is compared to biochemical replication by André Green in "Répétition, Différence, Réplication," *Revue Française de Psychanalyse,* 3, Tome XXXIV (1970), 461-501.

[61]Kristéva, *Polylogue,* p. 444.

[62]Kristéva's entire work opposes "le symbolique" to what she calls "le sémiotique." Her most lucid and complete presentation of the distinction is in *La Révolution du langage poétique,* pp. 17-100.

[63]Kristéva, *La Révolution du langage poétique,* p. 23.

[64]For an expanded discussion of this intellectual capacity, see Jonathan Culler, "Literary Competence," in *Reader-Response Criticism: From Formalism to Post-Structuralism,* ed. Jane P. Tompkins (Baltimore & London: Johns Hopkins University Press, 1980), pp. 101-17; also, his "Prolegomena to a Theory of Reading," in Inge Crosman and Susan R. Suleiman, eds., *The Reader in the Text: Essays on Audience and Interpretation* (Princeton: Princeton University Press, 1980), pp. 44-66.

[65]Sigmund Freud, "The Uncanny," in *Standard Edition,* 17, 219-56. As Freud demonstrates, this is a feeling one gets whenever something different turns out to be a repetition of the familiar. His proof is based on the etymology of the German word *heimlich* whose meaning coincides with its opposite *unheimlich.*

[66]Michael Riffaterre, *Essais de stylistique structurale* (Paris: Flammarion, 1970), p. 46.

[67]"Potential" because if it is found in a "non-literary" work (by our provisional definition, a work not accepted as literary by the vast majority of academics and scholars), it will not be accorded this aesthetic status.

[68]Cf. J. Hillis Miller's comment in *Fiction and Repetition,* p. 9: "The second [type of repetition, *intratextual* (my term)] is not the negation or opposite of the first, but its "counterpart" in a *strange relation* whereby the second is the subversive ghost of the first [*intertextual*] always already present within it as a possibility which hallows it out" (emphasis mine).

[69]Riffaterre, *La Production du texte,* pp. 45-60.

[70]Riffaterre, *Semiotics of Poetry*, p. 19.

[71]Roman Jakobson, *Essais de linguistique générale* (Paris: Editions de Minuit, 1963), p. 248.

[72]This is no doubt an utopian dream, since texts never drop from the sky, but are instead always already packaged in editions, critical essays, classrooms, and the like. Hence, they do have certain conventional aspects which are often noted at the very start of the reading act.

[73]For similar incompatibilities, see Riffaterre, *La Production du texte,* pp. 217-49.

[74]They have the same number of letters (9), many of which are in the same order: "o . . . lles."

[75]In his *Cornet à Dés* (Paris: Gallimard, 1945), p. 50, Max Jacob wrote a long poem entitled "Le Coq et la Perle," the very first paragraph of which contains the word *coquille.* Since pearls come from shells, nothing seems amiss with this poem at first glance. But moving from sea or shell code to barnyard animal code (*coq*) would be a much less obvious or justified transition without the graphemic similarity between the two terms. This random example already suggests, therefore, the closeness of the two terms in at least one formal paradigm.

[76]Perhaps the biggest difference between modern literary criticism and more traditional criticism lies in the former's emphasis on the *plurality* of these patterns at work in a text.

[77]The study of poeticity is thus equivalent, from the point of view developed here, to a systematic analysis of how "literary" style, as opposed to "non-literary style," is perceived by most critics.

Chapter II

INTERTEXTUAL REPETITIONS

A poetic or stylistic feature of a text is most often understood as a copy of something else, something which can be minimally described in linguistic terms. It is possible to distinguish between stylistic features on the basis of when and where their models are first perceived in the reading act: either the models are situated within the text's margins, or else they appear to derive directly from external sources. By definition then, intertextual repetitions involve previously fixed, socially recognizable models that are more or less copied by particular facets of a work.[1] If we say, "more or less," it is not because true repetition does not actually take place when we claim it does. It is rather that, remembering U. Eco's comment in this regard, an individual reader judges a textual feature a copy when it repeats certain pertinent features of a model that he can personally recover.

Since the judge or reader in this case is myself, perception of intertextual phenomena is contingent on my linguistic competence, and especially my literary competence. In order that I perceive them, I must be aware of various reading conventions, such as the law of what Culler calls "metaphorical coherence" (the attempt to produce coherence on the levels of both tenor and vehicle); or of the conventions that allow me to inscribe a poem in a specific tradition, or that force me to evaluate a particular thematic unity.[2] Though my own literary competence is perforce limited, it is not necessarily less pertinent than that of any other literary critic.

For these reasons, no one can ever pretend to do a global reading of all possible intertextuality in the three prose poem collections under analysis here. The farthest one can hope to go in this direction is to gather several samples from various categories of intertextual repetitions one observes throughout the corpus. In order to establish a preliminary typology of intertextuality, it is therefore indispensable to develop these categories one by one, and show how our three poets in turn illustrate their operation.

From the example of *Poisson soluble* no. 11 we can deduce three major rubrics under which to classify different types of intertextual repetition. The first covers the area most crucial to the reading act: the work in its entirety. This reading-space will be called the *discursive* level, where the work's total structure, upon a complete[3] linear reading, reminds one of other texts he has experienced before. It suffices to have read the surrealist prose of another author, for instance, to recognize the genre of Breton's poem no. 11. What this simple example suggests is that, in literature, certain general signs often combine to form useful critical labels, labels whose names vary from epic poem to sonnet to classical play. Of course, the prose poem as a whole does not give itself away quite as readily as do those other genres, in part, because it does not have as long a history. That is to say, there is nothing about the former that differentiates it *a priori* from, say, random pages of prose excerpted from a novel. Even so, my reading will demonstrate that some, if not most, of the peculiarity of prose poems results from their repeating formal aspects of well-known discourses or genres.

After this first kind of intertextual repetition (discursive) is perceived, and assuming one feels that a smaller textual unity repeats something one has read or heard before, the formal model copied is necessarily more subtle. As the text in *Poisson soluble* demonstrated, the copy may also come from common syntactical structures encountered elsewhere, such as those found in comparisons, clichés, descriptive systems, sterotypes, and even famous quotations that have been distorted or left incomplete. In this instance, one's simple linguistic competence is frequently all one needs in order to recover the model. Whenever it is not, one's literary competence must enter into the reading. Irrespective of the requisite competence, however, this second type of repetition, *phrasal*, always unfolds on the sentence level.

The final part of a literary work apt to make the reader recall a past model is the *lexical* level. Here, one or two words (or even fragments of a word, e.g., *rond* and *elles*), being stable units of a lexicon, have the potential to repeat two kinds of models. First, they recall the denotations and connotations of that cultural unit in the dictionary, native-speaker responses, and literary history. Secondly, they may repeat something more, something Derrida named the *supplément*. Without a doubt, this type of repetition (lexical) is the most pervasive, if not evident, type of intertextuality. Without it no one could ever string together any words at all. In consequence, some might consider "lexical repetition" a needlessly arcane appellation for the meaning of a given word.

But owing to its elusive nature, a word's "meaning" (the ultimate signified of a signifier) is just one side of, or reason for, its affiliation with other elements in the signifying chain that constitutes a work. Hence, when even a single lexical item—for reasons understandable only *a posteriori*— reminds the reader of what is *not* the text in front of him, he can be assured that it repeats some intertextual model. While it is intrinsic to his linguistic competence, this model need not strictly figure into the word's dictionary meaning alone. A good example is the morpheme *elles*, which, although not a denotation of *rondelles*, works along with it to signify something extra. The uncanny feeling the reader has at that point acts as both a proof of intertextuality,[4] and as a source for some portion of the text's poeticity.

I cannot insist enough that these three kinds of repetitions; discursive, phrasal, and lexical, are literary features whose purpose is to re-present, and, at the same time, differ from (or defer) fixed, external models or paradigms.[5] For such is the paradoxical nature of the phenomenon that repetition cannot exist without difference, but neither can difference exist without repetition.[6] Whenever we are confronted with an intertextual repetition, therefore, it automatically means that two *different* texts are involved; one present, the other absent. Certain aspects (paradigms) of the absent text are repeated, while others are negated or somehow converted. Shlomith Rimon-Kenon summarizes this whole state of affairs in one succinct statement: ". . . to repeat successfully is not to repeat."[7] Perfect repetition, in other words, is little more than the deliberate, mechanical replacement of an absent element into a present text, as in the case where a text, by means of quotation marks or collage, reproduces an exact phrase or word we know from somewhere else.

Thus, because one never finds a perfect intertextual repetition, the examples that follow cannot help but be "imperfect." Their so-called imperfections arise from the difference between the copy's present form, and formal environment, and its model's past. That there are any copies at all probably results from a dialectic between the author's desire to forget what he already knows, and his apparent inability to do so. Yet regardless of whether these different forms be purposeful or unintentional, their effective existence is much more the reader's affair than it is the author's. There is, after all, a certain amount of active participation or competence required to detect them.

Discursive Repetitions

If the discursive side of a work is the one most easily identified with "literary" traditions, then Baudelaire's "Les bons chiens" reflects how quite a few prose poems function. What is the paradigm or discursive intertextual model which the whole of "Les bons chiens" repeats? Several clues give the reader the idea that a specific genre antedating the text generates its structure. In the opening paragraph the narrator calls out for aid to help him sing[8] his nascent text. Addressing himself first to Buffon, a serious writer of natural history, he quickly changes his mind and takes Laurence Sterne as his literary support. This *farceur incomparable* is implored to inspire the narrator's song about "good" dogs, dogs he then paradoxically qualifies as being old, mangy, excrement-smeared, and property of the poor.

If it had not already been obvious before this point, the *anti*-ode form becomes so when we read, "Arrière la muse académique! Je n'ai que faire

de cette vieille bégueule. J'invoque la muse familière, la citadine, la vivante ..."
What Baudelaire has done here is to stand the tradition of the ode on its
head, and to remove the shroud of awe and grandeur from the practice of
extolling a given subject. Through a repetition of "odic language," in which
every positive aspect of high-class dogs ("danois, kingcharles, carlin...") is
converted into a negative one, e.g., "carlin ou gredin," and every negative
aspect of the everyday variety into a positive one, the author is able to
sustain his récit.

Now even though this language's most stereotypical dimensions—the
invocation of a muse, the historico-geographical setting of its action, the
"universal" admiration accorded its subjects—are in fact repeated, we say
there is discursive intertextual repetition only inasmuch as the selections
within these paradigms are opposite to those expected. As a result, the
author will: 1) denigrate the conventionally esteemed source of inspiration,
the Muse, and tell her to stand back; 2) situate his character in a kitchen or
in uninspiring Belgium, instead of in Greece or Rome (those mythologically
powerful visions so ingrained in the French sociolect); and 3) choose for
his subject matter filthy dogs, instead of a personage like Henri II,[9] or even a
noble creature like a nightingale.[10] Traces of the strict triadic form (strophe,
metrically identical antistrophe, and epode) are also present, but only as
violations[11] of the ode's rules:

Reconstructed Ode

Strophe -   "Où vont les chiens?" disait autrefois Nestor
               Roqueplan dans un immortel feuilleton qu'il a
               sans doute oublié, et dont moi seul, et Sainte-
               Beuve peut-être, nous nous souvenons encore
               aujourd'hui.

Antistrophe - Où vont les chiens, dites-vous, hommes peu
               attentifs? Ils vont à leurs affaires.

Epode -   Rendez-vous d'affaires, rendez-vous d'amour.
               A travers la brume, à travers la neige, à travers la
               crotte, sous la canicule mordante, sous la pluie
               ruisselante, ils vont, ils viennent, ils trottent, ils
               passent sous les voitures, excités par les puces, la
               passion, le besoin ou le devoir. Comme nous, ils
               se sont levés de bon matin, et ils cherchent leur
               vie ou courent à leurs plaisirs.

The repeated presence of this odic "ghost" is so strong that a reader of textual forms should thus have no problems in deciphering the semiotic conversion[12] which "Les bons chiens" puts into operation. Though negativized in this particular text, the encomiastic tradition provides Baudelaire with an effective framework that he then employs in a personal or idiolectic way. No less great a predecessor than Erasmus, we remember, did likewise with his *In Praise of Folly*.[13]

Turning now to the *Illuminations*, I direct my attention to the text "Dévotion":

DEVOTION

A ma soeur Louise Vanaen de Voringhen:—Sa cornette bleue tournée à la mer du Nord.—Pour les naufragés.

A ma soeur Léonie Aubois d'Ashby. Baou—l'herbe d'été bourdonnante et puante.—Pour la fièvre des mères et des enfants.

A Lulu,—démon—qui a conservé un goût pour les oratories du temps des Amies et de son éducation incomplète. Pour les hommes!—A Madame* * *.

A l'adolescent que je fus. A ce saint vieillard, ermitage ou mission.

A l'esprit des pauvres. Et à un très haut clergé.

Aussi bien, à tout culte en telle place de culte mémoriale et parmi tels événements qu'il faille se rendre, suivant les aspirations du moment ou bien notre propre vice sérieux.

Ce soir, à Circeto des hautes glaces, grasse comme le poisson, et enluminée comme les dix mois de la nuit rouge—(son coeur ambre et spunk),—pour ma seule prière muette comme ces régions de nuit, et précédant des bravoures plus violentes que ce chaos polaire.

A tout prix et avec tous les airs, même dans des voyages métaphysiques.—Mais plus *alors*.

As will be demonstrated shortly, the title itself is actually a *lexical* intertextual copy.[14] "Dévotion" *qua* lexeme brings to the reading-space all those cultural units with which it is associated: devotion to work, devotion to a country, devotion to a particular person, children, or God. Upon a rapid reading, however, none of the aforementioned units is more clearly actualized than the one signifying *religious* devotions. The syntactic model, *to x for y*, so typical of prayer and supplication, recurs throughout the text.

Still, the form of these religious devotions exhibits certain anomalous traits. Whereas the first nine copies respect this syntactic pattern by listing various individuals or groups to whom the prayers are directed, the people in question are hardly specific enough to pin down. As if the identities of Louise Vanaen de Voringhem, Léonie Aubois d'Ashby and Lulu were not already puzzling enough for the biographical critic, the narrator even throws in a madame *** to complete the mystery.

When we affirm that these personages are not specific, it does not preclude the fact that critics have spent hours trying to figure out just who they are.[15] Morphologically speaking, the women's names hint at the nationalities of the first two at least: (-inghem) Belgian, Dutch, or German; (Aubois d'Ashby) French and probably English. Be that as it may, one would be hard pressed to decide with any assuredness who Lulu is, which "saint vieillard, ermitage ou mission" is meant, and what "l'adolescent que je fus," "l'esprit des pauvres," or "un très haut clergé" refer to exactly.

The ensuing confusion[16] reaches its paroxysm when Rimbaud opts for words whose referentiality poses a never-ending enigma: *Baou, Circeto,* and *spunk.* It is true, as philologists are quick to point out, that in certain languages and dialects these terms do have distinct meanings. Even so, it would be difficult to dispute the fact that part of their semiotic function here consists in occulting the addressees (*destinataires*) of these devotions. While the referents continue to multiply, the reader, caught in an obscurity similar to that of liturgical rituals, grasps less and less of what is going on:

> "Aussi bien à tout culte en telle place de culte mémoriale et parmi tels événements qu'il faille se rendre, suivant les aspi-rations du moment ou bien notre propre vice sérieux.

The text thereby makes it increasingly evident that these devotions are meant for anyone or anything whatsoever, not for someone in particular.[17]

This generalized vagueness is further exacerbated when the prayers are said for the benefit of (*pour*) heterogeneous objects and people: the shipwrecked, the fever of mothers and children, men, and finally, the narrator's own *seule prière muette.* Remarkably, this last item permits the poem to go full circle and come back upon itself, for now the narrator is praying in order to be able to pray! By dint of repeating *to x for y,* "Dévotion" thus copies the discourse of a litany.

Yet our reading does not stop there. The real coup de grâce is delivered by the last word, *alors.* Because this word is italicized in the text, the reader's eyes are drawn to its particular shape. Seeing that the anaphoric preposition *à* is the one blatant formal aspect structuring the entire work, it is reasonable to read this word as the ultimate expression (within this context) of indeterminacy: *a & lors*, "to that (unknown) time." Although the adverb's etymology alone justifies such a division, the poem's discursive intertextual repetition overdetermines it. Critics who put more weight on meaning than form will usually miss this kind of scriptural possibility. Some even go so far as to suggest that Rimbaud really made a mistake, that he had meant to write "mais plus *maintenant*" instead of *alors*.

As much as we may want to change the words, we have no good reason to tamper with the author's choices. Indeed, the line just before this last syntagm commences the very transcendental movement that our suggested *à & lors* would express: "A tout prix et avec tous les airs, même dans des voyages métaphysiques." In the wake of a long list of addressees, whose semantic inter-relationships were already tenuous, the reader begins to understand that a temporal beyond is the one convenient closing for this extraordinary devotion. At that unknown time, he rationalizes, there will literally be more, *plus*, to pray for.

Since this realm of the not-now (*lors*) is the maximally uncertain entity, it cannot be counted on to answer prayers, even if they be of the type earlier addressed to ephemeral characters, like madame ***. As nothing about that realm is yet known, the most the narrator can do is to allude to it in the proper devotional idiom, *à*. The rest of his prayer is necessarily mute, and therefore ends.

Part of the stylistic efficacy of the morpheme *lors* derives from its repeating the graphemic shape of the first three addressees in the poem: Louise, Léonie, and Lulu. Thanks to its terminal position it acts as the refrain or coda for "Dévotion." A framing-technique common to many other literary texts thereby sees the light. Beginning and ending in the devotional "mode," Rimbaud's poem is a devotion for devotion's sake, a devotion that would have us recognize in it a new literary genre.

His text "Solde" functions similarly. Copying the form of a list of items for sale, it looks as if it included bona fide articles of interest to prospective buyers. But in the mythological terms of the French sociolect, nothing is in fact for sale: "A vendre ce que les Juifs n'ont pas vendu, ce que noblesse ni crime n'ont goûté, ce qu'ignorent l'amour maudit et la probité infernale des masses. . . ." It is a sale for the sake of a sale.

The first text in André Breton's collection, *Poisson soluble*, opens with a sentence that immediately informs the reader of the type of literature he is about to read: "Le parc, à cette heure, étendait ses mains blondes au-dessus de la fontaine magique."[18] Knowing that real parks do not behave this way, and that magic fountains do not exist, he automatically relates what follows to the discourse of fairy tales or other fantastic stories.[19] Because it respects no metrical pattern, the subsequent details are presented as so many aspects of a would-be *fantaisie*, defined as an "oeuvre d'imagination, dans laquelle la création artistique n'est généralement pas soumise à des règles formelles" (*Le Petit Robert*). The action moves from a château to an inn, then back to a woman in the château. Finally it revolves around the notion of an escape (*fuite*), as well as the woman's departure by horse ("l'ombre ici présente est sortie tantôt à cheval"). A phantom seems intent on tracking her down.

Although the extraordinary details (e.g., "Un château sans signification roulait à la surface de la terre") can be seen as a necessary dimension of this surrealist narrative, their particularity disconcerts the reader the further along he gets. What is there about the inn's name, *Au Baiser de la jeune Veuve,* or about the woman's origin, *la jeune Irlandaise*, for instance, that makes them appropriate and not gratuitous choices for this tale? Is there anything about *les oiseaux de mer* per se that explains their qualification as, "filles du sépulchre bleu, jours de fête, formes sonnées de l'angélus de mes yeux et de ma tête quand je m'éveille, usages des provinces flammées . . .?" Does the age of the phantom introduced (two hundred years) matter or not?

Since Breton's *Manifeste* was written in the same year as this collection, we can assume that the extraordinariness of this text's images derives in part from their being samples of the surreal. We recall that the description of Surrealism included in the *Manifeste* linked the movement and its ideas with nineteenth-century Supernaturalism. Suddenly, the Supernaturalist work to which Breton drew a surrealist parallel, Nerval's *Les Filles du Feu*, reveals itself to be the key to, or "interpretant" for, this text's poeticity. In the earlier work, one finds a chapter[20] devoted to a young Irish woman named "Jemmy," that contains all the narrative elements of the present prose poem. Let us see how.

In Nerval's story, the young Irish woman meets a man at a *maison du rendez-vous* in the American wilderness (Breton will describe her as a "plant de vigne américain"). In a short time, she marries him. One day the unfortunate woman decides to ride an extremely large horse that leaves her stranded, and at the mercy of an Indian, who keeps her with him for five years. At the end of this period, she cleverly escapes (cf. the repeated substantive *fuite* in Breton's poem), and returns to her husband. He has remarried, leaving her no other options than to leave him again (hence, the young "widow"). She then goes back into the woods. The great majority of details in the automatic text thus copy narrative models from the chapter entitled "Jemmy."

Yet we still do not know what to make of the phantom, or of certain other details regarding the woman. Having discovered this important connection to Nerval, one need not look very far in order to attain the necessary clarification. A well known poem of his, which happens to have as its title the word "Fantaisie,"[21] reveals the extent to which Breton's fantasy depends on the earlier corpus:

> Il est un air pour qui je donnerais
> Tout Rossini, tout Mozart et tout Weber
> Un air très vieux, languissant et funèbre,
> Qui pour moi seul a des charmes secrets.
>
> Or, chaque fois que je viens à l'entendre,
> *De deux cents ans mon âme rajeunit:*
> C'est sous *Louis-Treize* . . .—Et je crois voir s'étendre
> Un coteau vert que le couchant jaunit;
>
> *Puis un château* de brique à coins de pierre,
> Aux vitraux teints de rougeâtres couleurs,
> *Ceint de grands parcs, avec une rivière*
> *Baignant ses pieds,* qui coule entre des fleurs.
>
> Puis *une dame, à sa haute fenêtre,*
> *Blonde* aux yeux noirs, en ses habits anciens . . .
> Que, dans une autre existence peut-être,
> J'ai déjà vue—et dont je me souviens! (emphasis mine)

From the age of this other phantom, to the location and description of the château, to the woman at the window, Nerval's poem generates a series of images which, though scrambled,[22] are present in Breton's writing. Thanks to its title, that intertextually repeats the type of discourse involved, it imposes itself onto the later poet's work as an exemplary instance of such fantasizing about women. Breton's almost obsessional concern here with women from an earlier epoch is further confirmed by the appearance in his text of Madame de Pompadour's shadow. Living two hundred years before him, the mistress of Louis XV could not be more suited to this liminary text of *Poisson soluble.* Her real name, we remember, was Madame Poisson. And since Breton's prose poem was written approximately one hundred years after Nerval's piece, it is perfectly consistent that Louis XV's shadow should be present in the former and Louis XIII in the latter. The two monarchs reigned approximately a century apart.

Notation of discursive repetition in our four prose poems is therefore the first step in any analysis of their poeticity. Once aware of the literary affiliation a text has, one can more easily identify other less extensive repetitive features. The examples that follow do not preclude, but rather presuppose this primary dimension of intertextuality.

Phrasal Repetitions

Perceiving an unmarked quotation requires partial, if not complete, knowledge of the original utterance. When one lacks this knowledge, the power or value of a direct quotation diminishes somewhat. Often, however, a reader comes across a phrase that reminds him not of something specific, but rather of a more general kind of linguistic structure. This structure, earlier called a "phantom," takes a myriad of shapes, depending on the text which surrounds it. Whenever someone utilizes such shapes, he does so on the assumption that the structure or referent to which he is alluding is equivalent to the one another person has described differently.

A case in point is the riddle; or more specifically, a series of riddles, the answers to which remain identical. From our perspective, literary sentences correspond to different riddles that beat around the same unnamed bush. They oblige the reader to deduce the one matrix (bush) that generates these riddles. The reason they make him behave thus is that in the same instant he reads a given phrase, words and phrases from other texts in his memory begin to re-surface. When enough of them converge onto one structure, the reader has recovered the copy's model. To that end, let us examine closely the way a present work repeats these temporarily lost syntagms; that is, how it copies a different form of a particular phrase.

Baudelaire's prose poem "Les Fenêtres" contains the following description:

> Il n'est pas d'objet plus profond, plus mystérieux,
> plus fécond, plus ténébreux, plus éblouissant qu'une [. . .].
> Dans ce trou noir ou lumineux vit la vie, rêve la
> vie, souffre la vie.

In order to maintain my riddle analogy, I have intentionally left out the object being described. This strategy permits me to demonstrate the role of phrasal repetition in answering this type of text-based question. In addition, it helps me show how such repetitions can cause a reading to go off track at one moment, while putting it back at another.

Most readers tend to fill in blanks like the above as they progress through a work. In ordinary conversations, people perform a similar operation whenever they say what their interlocutors are about to say, the word(s) the others were "looking for." Yet, on occasion, the reader makes an error in his prediction. Upon a first reading of "Les Fenêtres," for example, it may unsettle some to discover that the object in question is a window lighted by a candle, not the sea. Recalling certain stereotypical images of the sea, it seems logical enough (to me, for one) to think that that is what the line describes. To clarify this point, consider some verses from one of the most celebrated sea poems in the French language, Valery's "Le Cimetière Marin":

> Quand sur l'abîme un soleil se repose
> Masse de calme et visible réserve,
> Eau sourcilleuse, Oeil qui gardes en toi
> Tant de sommeil sous un voile de flamme . . .[23]

In these four lines alone are found exemplary substantives for two of the adjectives in Baudelaire's sentence: the abyss (*profond*), the sun and flaming veil (*éblouissant*).

An even more telling model for his prose poem sentence can be recovered from Baudelaire's own, "L'homme et la mer," a verse piece in *Les Fleurs du Mal*:

> Vous êtes tous les deux ténébreux et discrets:
> Homme, nul n'a sondé le fond de tes abîmes;
> O mer, nul ne connaît tes richesses intimes,
> Tant vous êtes jaloux de garder vos secrets!

In this single strophe, every element of the "prosaic" copies in "Les Fenêtres" finds a poetic prototype. The attributes associated with men and the sea in the poem correspond to those of the windows in the prose poem. Moreover, this shift from man to windows is justified by the rest of the latter text, since it is a contemplation of the person's life *behind* these panes of glass that really interests the narrator, not a contemplation of the glass. Opting for a concrete entity (windows), rather than one which might quickly lead to abstraction (*M*an), Baudelaire shies away from a metaphoric idiom that would be more appropriate in poetic verses about mankind.[24]

This repetition of sea imagery would not amount to much if the word "sea" did not somehow figure in the rest of the text. No matter how accurate the description may be, we must not forget that, in this text, it still refers to the "wrong" object, a window. It thus produces a catachresis. The relevant question here is whether the appearance of sea stereotypes is gratuitous or not. Does the text retrieve this unsaid referent, or does it merely lead the reader further and further astray? The start of the second paragraph gives us one brief glimpse at what we thought was the answer to Baudelaire's riddle-like phrase: "Par-delà des vagues de toits, j'aperçois une femme mûre, ridée déjà. . . ." Instead of simply reporting the presence of roofs, the narrator introduces the image, "vagues de toits." Situated in the first textual slot after the window description, this metaphor of waves of roofs could easily go unnoticed were it not for the initial phrasal repetition of marine stereotypes.

The reason why this metaphor might not be stressed by most readers is that, seen from high above a city, a wide expanse of roofs (as well as the city in its entirety) has been described in many other texts in terms of its undulatory character. When the observer has an elevated vantage point, a "literary" city will frequently take on the allure of the sea. In Baudelaire's "Paysage," for example, the narrator implicitly compares the city below him to a ship in the middle of an ocean:

> Les deux mains au menton, du haut de ma mansarde,
> Je verrai l'atelier qui chante et qui bavarde;
> Les tuyaux, les clochers, ces *mâts* de la cité,
> Et les grands ciels qui font rêver d'éternité. (emphasis mine)

From his bird's eye view, Hugo informs us that in medieval Paris,

> on voyait, par places, percer, dans cette *mer de maisons,* quelques groupes de tours en ruine des anciennes enceintes, comme les pitons de collines *dans une inondation,* comme des *archipels* du vieux Paris *submergé* sous le nouveau[25] (emphasis mine).

An inversion of the association, roofs ←→ sea, can also be noted in the first verse of Valéry's "Le Cimetière Marin": "Ce toit tranquille où marchent les colombes. . . ." In conclusion, then, the apparently trivial metaphor, *vagues de toits*, becomes a suitable, even exemplary, literary device in this prose poem by recovering an important seme (waves) from the unsaid sea of our earlier sentence. Although the reader may end up unconvinced of the relative aesthetic merits of the syntagm, he can at least admire the subtlety of its semiotic role here.

Descriptive systems, or what we might call stereotypical descriptions, like the one we have just seen, transcend a significant number of cultural barriers. That is to say, other passages from English, German, or Spanish literature would have worked equally well in proving my point about sea imagery. Unlike specific references to the fixed units of a sociolect, such stereotypes are often shared by more than a single nationality or race, making them similar to Jungian archetypes. In certain texts, though, one happens upon a phrase that rings a particular bell in one's memory, a bell attached as it were to something peculiar to the language and/or literature of that reader's society alone. The problems in elucidating these idiomatic expressions or clichés, and in indicating the sources of various famous lines are among the most arduous tasks of translation. The translator knows that to carry over the proper form of this type of utterance into another language is sometimes an impossible feat. The graphemic, phonemic, not to mention semantic character of the work often suffers substantial and irreparable alteration in the process.

Through the narrative expansion of a common French expression, Baudelaire's "Le Mauvais Vitrier" illustrates this very principle of inviolability we find in literary discourse. Though it never explicitly states it, the entire text repeats the phrase, *casser les vitres*, a figurative expression meaning "to cause a scandal or ruckus." What the author does is take those words to the letter. He recounts a story about a glazier who is equipped with various panes of glass (*vitres*), and who walks the streets in hopes of making a sale. The narrator, described as one of those "natures purement contemplatives et tout à fait impropres à l'action," calls him up to his apartment in order to examine his wares. After inspecting the glass, the normally placid narrator flies into a rage and screams:

> "Comment? vous n'avez pas de verres de couleur? des verres roses, rouges, bleus, des vitres magiques, des vitres de paradis? Impudent que vous êtes! vous osez vous promener dans des quartiers pauvres, et vous n'avez pas même de vitres qui fassent voir la vie en beau!"

Scandalized by the glazier's lack of joy-producing colored glass (the preferred color being pink, as in another French expression, *voir la vie en rose*, that signifies looking on the sunny side of life), he then creates his own scandal. He shoves the unlucky victim down the stairs, breaking all his glass. Indifferent to the glazier's fate, he puts his usual tranquility completely aside, and he says, "ivre de ma folie, je lui criai furieusement: 'La vie en beau! La vie en beau!' " The two meanings in French of the words "breaking the glass" are thus fused into one by means of this three-page prose poem.[26]

Outside of a strictly French context, the title of Rimbaud's "Après le Déluge" presents no problem of interpretation. As a reference to the time period that follows the biblical flood, it conjures up the vision of a newly cleansed, reborn world. But for the reading public that shares the text's language, it also copies the well-known phrase, "Après moi, le Déluge!"[27] I could express the meaning of the last phrase in this fashion: "After me, and for all I care, the Flood can happen again; my only concern is with the present." Given this intertextual model, the syntagm formed by the title is slightly problematic. Does the author mean after *the* Flood, or after a metaphorical flood or catastrophe that would follow his own life ("Après *moi*")? Is he writing about the past or the future?

The answer to these questions is never revealed, as the first line merely exacerbates our uncertainty: "Aussitôt que l'*idée* du Déluge se fut rassise" (emphasis mine). Making an abstraction (*idée*) out of what was supposed to be history's single greatest disaster is equivalent to undermining its status as an actual event.[28] Yet in stating that this idea "sits back down," the text describes the abstract in terms of the concrete. If the idea sits down again (*rassise*), it is a sign that this tremendous cleansing has very probably happened before, or will happen again. In fact, the poem ends with the narrator imploring the Flood*s* (*les Déluges*) to wash everything away again.

Since the biblical Flood signaled the end of one world and the beginning of another, the "idea" of it has to be that of an enormous catharsis and rebirth. The entire text could be said to develop out of the concept of an *after*math. The exact moment (in the past or in the future) of the aftermath's inception is uncertain, but not the idea of it. So the one thing we are sure of, in the light of the phrasal repetition, is that the scene transpires *afterwards*. Every person, every creature, goes back to what he was starting to do before the onrush of the waters: "les étals se dressèrent," "l'on tira les barques vers la mer," "Les 'mazagrans' fumèrent dans les estaminets," "Dans la grande maison de vitres encore ruisselante les enfants regardèrent les merveilleuses images," "les caravanes partirent."

The child-like innocence of the animals and natural surroundings underlines the fresh, new-born quality of this recently cleansed world:

> Un lièvre s'arrêta dans les sainfoins et les clochettes
>   mouvantes et dit sa prière à l'arc-en-ciel à travers la toile
>   de l'araignée,
> Oh! les pierres précieuses qui se cachaient, -les fleurs qui
>   regardaient déjà [. . .]
> Puis, dans la futaie violette, bourgeonnante, Eucharis me
>   dit que c'était le printemps. . . .

What comes *after* (but when?) is depicted, therefore, as a series of different forms of renewal: renewal of commerce, of social life, and of nature itself. Because we do not know what has not yet happened, i.e., "le déluge après moi," Rimbaud describes it in the language of a new start. The text's conclusion summarizes the entire situation: "la Reine, la Sorcière qui allume sa braise dans le pot de terre, ne voudra jamais nous raconter ce qu'elle sait, et que nous ignorons." The Witch who is starting her fire will never want to tell us what she knows (the future). For this reason, we will continue to be ignorant of what comes *after*. We can only understand in terms of what comes before.[29]

Clichés, which are included in any native speaker's vocabulary, can also function as constitutive elements of poeticity. Our example this time is no. 23 of *Poisson soluble*:

> Tu sauras plus tard, quand je ne vaudrai plus la pluie pour me pendre, quand le froid, appuyant ses mains sur les vitres, là où une étoile bleue n'a pas encore tenu son rôle, à la lisière d'un bois, viendra dire à toutes celles qui me resteront fidèles sans m'avoir connu: "C'était un beau capitaine, galons d'herbes et manchettes noires, un mécanicien peut-être qui rendait la vie pour la vie. Il n'avait pas d'ordres à faire exécuter pour cela, c'eût été trop doux, mais la fin de ses rêves était la signification à donner aux mouvements de la Balance céleste qui le faisait puissant avec la nuit, misérable avec le jour. Il était loin de partager vos joies et vos peines; il ne coupait pas la poire en quatre. C'était un beau capitaine. Dans ses rayons de soleil il entrait plus d'ombre que dans l'ombre, mais il ne brunit vraiment qu'au soleil de minuit. Les cerfs l'étourdissaient dans les clairières, surtout les cerfs blancs dont les cors sont d'étranges instruments de musique. Il dansait alors, il veillait à la libre croissance des fougères dont les crosses blondes se détendent depuis dans vos cheveux. Peignez pour lui vos cheveux, peignez-les sans cesse, il ne demande pas autre chose. Il n'est plus là mais il va revenir, il est peut-être déjà revenu, ne laissez pas une autre puiser à la fontaine: s'il revenait, ce serait sans doute par là. Peignez vos cheveux à la fontaine et qu'ils inondent avec elle la plaine." Et tu verras dans les entrailles de la terre, tu me verras plus vivant que je ne suis à cette heure où le sabre d'abordage du ciel me menace. Tu m'entraîneras plus loin qu'où je n'ai pu aller, et tes bras seront des grottes hurlantes de jolies bêtes et d'hermines. Tu ne feras de moi qu'un soupir, qui se poursuivra à travers tous les Robinsons de la terre. Je ne suis pas perdu pour toi: je suis seulement à l'écart de ce qui te ressemble, dans les hautes mers, là où l'oiseau nommé Crève-Coeur pousse son cri qui élève les pommeaux de glace dont les astres du jour sont la garde brisée.

Thanks to a scrambling of two clichés, the opening line forms a structural matrix that will be repeated by the rest of the poem: "Tu sauras plus tard, quand je ne vaudrai plus la pluie pour me pendre. . . ." The scrambled clichés subtending this matricial phrase are, *Il ne vaut pas la corde pour le pendre*, and *Il pleut des cordes*. Substituting the rain of the second expression for the rope in the first, Breton succeeds in creating an exemplary surrealist image. An approximate English translation of this image would read something like, "You'll understand later, when I am no longer worth the rain to hang myself with. . . ."

As often happens in automatic texts, this preliminary find (*trouvaille*) gives birth to additional copies patterned after it. Remembering our earlier theoretical stance on the interdependence of a poem's inside and outside, i.e., elements *in praesentia* and *in absentia*, everything is as it should be. The formal matrix, Distorted Clichés, goes on to produce these phrases of note: "toutes celles qui me resteront fidèles *sans* m'avoir connu," instead of the more logical *après m'avoir connu;* "un mécanicien qui rendait la vie pour la vie," rather than *le mal pour le mal;* "il ne coupait pas la poire en quatre," a scrambling of *couper la poire en deux, se couper en quatre*, and *couper les cheveux en quatre;* and finally, "Dans ses rayons de soleil," not *Dans le soleil de sa gloire* or *Dans les rayons de sa gloire*.

Furthermore, this phrasal repetition spreads to smaller and smaller segments of sentences, overlapping as it were the category of lexical intertextuality we shall develop next: "les astres du jour," which alters the common singular form, *l'astre du jour,* meaning the sun; "soleil de minuit," when the sole possibility for the sun tan in question is *soleil de midi;* "puiser à la fontaine," not the more usual *puiser à la source;* "les entrailles de la terre," not *les entrailles du sol;* and last and most telling of all, "tous les Robinsons de la Terre." If ever there were a noun that bespoke solitariness and singularity it would have to be Robinson Crusoe. Yet here, conforming to Breton's idiolect (Distortion), it must be pluralized.

While the narrator of this typical "sour grapes" letter speaks in clichés—warning his lover that someday she will regret hearing others say, "C'était un beau capitaine . . ." (another cliché)—his knowledge of them, as we can see, is hopelessly inadequate. Even so, his stylistic strategy, which consists of modifying their proper forms, does lend a sort of credibility to his sincerity. The implication is that he, unlike experts in the field of clichés, is an exceptional victim of this platitudinous, amorous situation. When he says, "je ne suis pas perdu pour toi: Je suis seulement à l'écart de ce qui te ressemble . . .", the reader has reason to interpret his remark as a metalinguistic comment on the writing itself. In effect, what this narrative voice would be expressing is its resemblance to, but separateness from, the series of clichés that constitutes the prose poem at hand.

Each imperfect repetition of these exemplary intertextual phrases, personified by the poem's subject, *Je,* would thus be apostrophizing the correct model, *Tu.*[30] His gaucheness, another familiar facet of the misbegotten lover's final plea for reconciliation, becomes the icon of his worthiness for love. And though he is lonely, like every other Robinson on earth, *Je* at least spares his beloved the boredom of a perfectly trite self-defense.

Lexical Repetitions

The description of a literary text proceeds from the gradual appraisal of its various formal dimensions: the grosser the level on which we recognize signs of poeticity, the greater our desire to concentrate on the work's finer levels. This progressive focusing is needed in order to substantiate any further claims we may wish to make about the literariness of a particular text. In other terms, from the moment a reader notices a discursive intertextual repetition, he begins scrutinizing those smaller unities (phrases, words) that uphold the bigger, more extensive discursive structure he has already identified.

Admittedly, the precise order in which this realization occurs cannot always be accurately determined. One could certainly argue, for instance, that the individual critic must first notice other types of repetition *before* deciding upon the genre it is repeating. If this objection were granted for the sake of argumentation, it would still be presumptuous to believe that such a chicken-or-egg controversy had much pertinence to the formal typology proposed here. I must therefore put aside the empirical question of the order in which stylistic features are perceived until our conclusion. At present, I am more interested in the relationship between these features than in the relative points at which they manifest themselves in the reading-act.

How many outside models do the lexical unities of a piece of literature repeat? In the first place, it is understood that the greatest portion of any poem's structure is contingent upon a repetition and intertwining of the definitions of its component words. The main reason for this is that all words have verifiable dictionary definitions. As a result, when I read this sentence from Baudelaire's "Le Joueur généreux," I automatically envisage two round, anatomical, visual instruments in the faces of these unfortunate people:

> Si je voulais essayer de définir d'une manière quelconque l'expression singulière de leurs regards, je dirais que jamais je ne vis d'yeux brillant plus énergiquement de l'horreur de l'ennui et du désir immortel de se sentir vivre.

Although my periphrasis affirms that I know something about the semantic fields normatively applied to the word "yeux," it does not necessarily facilitate the attribution of any "poetic" quality to it. The denotations of these eyes, in other words, are not distinguishable from the ones I might expect to find in a sociological treatise on the subject.

Yet as the text unfolds, the memory of these eyes, and of the particular syntagm in which they are situated, becomes increasingly relevant to our reading. By signifying both what the dictionary tells us they do, and, *at the same time,* something more, they perform a distinctly literary function. To see exactly how our poet accomplishes this, it is essential to gather more contextual information. The tale is set in an underground home. The narrator visits this home at the request of a mysterious Being. More specifically, the request comes in the form of a "clignement d'oeil significatif," which he hastens to obey. (One will soon get the impression that everything significant in this prose poem takes place at eye level.) Upon entering this home, described as "éblouissante, où éclatait un luxe dont aucune des habitations supérieures de Paris ne pourrait fournir un exemple approchant," the narrator says that one "y respirait une béatitude sombre." This beatitude is then compared to the lugubrious stupor experienced by the lotus eaters. As such, the adjective "sombre" is figuratively taken to mean "gloomy." But within the context of this dazzling or splendiferous abode, "sombre" must also be understood in its literal sense of "dark." After all, the enchanted island of the lotus eaters to which Baudelaire alludes is qualified as being "éclairée des lueurs d'une éternelle après-midi." Through a repetition of this dark-bright opposition, the text thus establishes a formal unity that will shortly be exposed as the conflict between God and the Devil. In the following words, this "generous player" will recall the tradition which associates the Devil with darkness and God with light:

> mes chers frères, n'oubliez jamais, quand vous entendrez vanter
> le progrès des lumières, que la plus belle des ruses du diable est
> de vous persuader qu'il n'existe pas.

In the course of this new version of the Homeric, Virgilian, and Dantean descent into the underworld, the narrator discovers many strange faces of men and women, "marqués d'une beauté fatale." Their presence does not, however, scare him away. Instead, they inspire in him a kind of fraternal sympathy. It is at this point that he tries to define what lies behind their expressions. When we reread the description, our attention is drawn to a specific syntagm, "jamais je ne vis *d'yeux* brillant plus énergiquement de l'horreur de l'ennui et du désir immortel de se sentir vivre [emphasis mine]." Now the eyes repeat not only conventional aspects (e.g., round organs of vision) of the signifier "eyes," they also bring along with those same features a phonemic *supplément* ("Dieu") that recalls the whole Derridean problematic of *différance*. We can no longer limit the signifier's "true" meaning to the sole denotative plane.

The point, of course, is that God fits in the context just as much as do the eyes in which the narrator "sees" him. Irreducible to a single signified, the syntagm *d'yeux* adds yet another layer of meaning to a text about the Devil.[31] And if the narrator never saw *God* shining more brightly than from out of this infernal place, that is precisely why he felt no fear in front of these strange faces.

Needless to say, each and every instance of the syntagm *d'yeux* does not play the same semiotic role it plays here.[32] If it did, we would have to discard the whole notion of orthography and replace it with fortuitous spelling. We are not recommending that anyone do that. Nevertheless, this example demonstrates what even minute signifying units are capable of when found in a literary text. Given certain stylistic and semantic environments, such formal phenomena attract the reader's attention and complement the other signifying structures in the poem. In addition to dictionary meanings, therefore, signifiers can assume idiosyncratic forms which simultaneously permit them to repeat other intertextual models. These models then invite the reader back into the present text in order to find the copies they put accordingly into a new light.

Rimbaud's "Fête d'hiver" gives rise to a similar, if less accurate phonemic doubling with the words *faits divers,*[33] those short anecdotal stories usually found in newspapers or periodicals:

> La cascade sonne derrière les huttes d'opéra-comique. Des girandoles prolongent, dans les vergers et les allées voisins du Méandre,—les verts et les rouges du couchant. Nymphes d'Horace coiffées au Premier Empire,—Rondes Sibériennes, Chinoises de Boucher.

Meandering from epoch to epoch (Antiquity, First Empire), culture to culture (Greece, Rome, France, Russia, China), and art to art (comic opera, rondelay, Boucher's Chinese women), this text, the shortest of the *Illuminations,* evokes a mass of anecdotal material that could become precisely innumerable *faits divers.* In that sense, the title acts both as a kind of pun and as a semiotic reminder of the journalistic genre *faits divers.* These two functions of lexical intertextual repetition will be more fully explained very shortly.

Baudelaire's "Le Port" too, exhibits a supplement-bearing tendency of literary lexemes, though not by way of phonemic contiguity:

Un port est un séjour charmant pour une âme fatiguée des luttes de la vie. L'ampleur du ciel, l'architecture mobile des nuages, les colorations changeantes de la mer, le scintillement des phares, sont un prisme merveilleusement propre à amuser les yeux sans jamais les lasser. Les formes élancées des navires, au gréement compliqué, auxquels la houle imprime des oscillations harmonieuses, servent à entretenir dans l'âme le goût du rythme et de la beauté. Et puis, surtout, il y a une sorte de plaisir mystérieux et aristocratique pour celui qui n'a plus ni curiosité ni ambition, à contempler, couché dans le belvédère ou accoudé sur le môle, tous ces mouvements de ceux qui partent et de ceux qui reviennent, de ceux qui ont encore la force de vouloir, le désir de voyager ou de s'enrichir.

While describing a port in a fashion consistent with its set denotations—the sea, lighthouse, ships—it also repeats that poetic usage of the word "port" which makes of it the metaphor for man's final destination, death. The text initiates this double expansion[34] from the very first line: "Un port est un séjour charmant pour une âme fatiguée des luttes de la vie." Because the soul is tired, it takes pleasure in the tranquility of the passing clouds and ships, the changing colors in the sea and sky, and harmonious motion of the waves.

Yet, to state that the soul is tired "des luttes de la vie" is to invoke several other literary instances where such fatigue portends the end of one's life. Think of the plethora of characters in Racine whose fates are sealed when they exclaim, "Hélas!", which means etymologically (hé + las), "Oh, I'm so unfortunate, and tired of it all. . . ." Or of Maeterlinck's verses:

> Mon âme en est triste à la fin;
> Elle est triste enfin d'être lasse,
> Elle est lasse enfin d'être en vain.[35]

Although the narrator in Baudelaire's poem never actually voices the term "death," his every word teems with its presence. He is "celui qui n'a plus ni curiosité ni ambition." He remains[36] as stationary as a dead man "couché dans le belvédère ou accoudé sur le môle," contemplating "tous ces mouvements de ceux qui partent et de ceux qui reviennent, de ceux qui ont encore la force de vouloir, le désir de voyager ou de s'enrichir." By copying two different models of the signifier "port," the text thus says one thing and means another.

Consequently, lexical intertextual repetitions have much in common with the classical trope *syllepsis:* "une figure par laquelle le même mot est pris tout-à-la-fois dans le sens propre et dans un sens figuré.[37] In the light of my first example (*d'yeux*), however, I must once again insist that the word's meaning (*sens*) is not so much at issue as is its form. For whenever one tries to put his finger on a literal or figurative meaning, his only recourse is to other words that *stand for* those meanings. Inevitably, these other words have different morphophonemic configurations from the ones they represent. In order then not to lose sight of potential formal features in literature (features included neither in literal nor figurative meanings), it would seem advisable to think of meaning itself as a particular form in a particular instant.[38]

With this perspective in mind, we no longer need to guess where the figurative begins and where the literal ends. As long as we can isolate a model elsewhere, i.e., an intertextual model, which justifies our reading a word in a given way, the word can legitimately be judged a copy of it. The copy's "true" pertinence, therefore, depends on the extent of its textual functionality. It works in direct proportion to the reader's willingness to pursue the repetition's repercussions throughout the text.

As mentioned earlier, puns, too, have their place among this type of lexical repetition. In "Portraits de Maîtresses," Baudelaire has one of the characters describe his mistress as a phenomenal beauty with one major flaw. She never succeeds in getting enough to eat. In his terms, "J'aurais pu faire ma fortune en la montrant dans les foires comme *monstre polyphage*. Je la nourrissais bien; et cependant elle m'a quitté. . . ." As we have already observed the usefulness of italics in a previous poem,[39] it should not surprise us that *polyphage* signifies in a special way. Though this "monster" eats practically everything, and at all times, she has a specific weakness for men. The linguistic structure supporting this lexical formal feature is the expression *mangeuse* or *dévoreuse d'hommes*, a well-known cliché for a ravishing woman. Possessing the same aggressivity that our "lady-killer" has vis-à-vis women, this cliché is the interpretant[40] that guides our reading of the words *monstre polyphage*.

The erotic overtones of her omnivorous behavior are then further underlined by the description of her next man, a man she will also probably "eat" some day. A friend wonders whether she left the first man for a *fournisseur aux vivres*. The mournful response is: "quelque chose d'approchant, une espèce d'employé dans l'intendance qui, par quelque tour de bâton à lui seul connu, fournit peut-être à cette pauvre enfant la ration de plusieurs soldats." With the aid of this tricky stick, does this employee give her several soldiers' rations, or does he give her the (sexual) equivalent of several soldiers *as* a ration? Given the context, we might assume the latter to be the case.

That one word can intertextually copy several models, and then become a model for intratextual copies, can also be observed in *Poisson soluble* no. 19.

> Entre la source. La source a parcouru la ville à la recherche d'un peu d'ombre. Elle n'a pas trouvé ce qu'il lui fallait, elle se plaint tout en racontant ce qu'elle a vu : elle a vu le soleil des lampes, plus touchant que l'autre, il est vrai; elle a chanté un ou deux airs à la terrasse d'un café et on lui a jeté de lourdes fleurs jaunes et blanches; elle a ramené ses cheveux sur son visage mais leur parfum était si fort. Elle n'est que trop portée à s'endormir, est-il bien nécessaire qu'elle couche à la belle étoile parmi ses colliers d'insectes, ses bracelets de verre? La source rit doucement, elle n'a pas senti ma main se poser sur elle; elle se courbe insensiblement sous ma main, pensant aux oiseaux qui ne veulent savoir d'elle que sa fraîcheur. Qu'elle prenne garde, je suis capable de l'entraîner bien ailleurs, là où il n'y a plus ni villes ni campagnes. Un beau mannequin présentera cet hiver aux élégantes la robe du Mirage et savez-vous qui fera triompher l'adorable création? Mais la source, bien sûr, la source que j'entraîne sans difficultés dans ces parages où mes idées reculent au-delà du possible, au-delà mêmes des sables inorganiques où les Touaregs, d'origine moins obscure que moi, se contentent d'une vie nomade parmi leurs femmes excessivement parées. La source, elle est tout ce qui passe de moi dans le tournoiement des feuilles qui veillent là-haut, au-dessus de mes idées mouvantes que le moindre courant d'air déplace, elle est l'arbre que la cognée attaque sans cesse, elle saigne dans le soleil et elle est le miroir de mes mots.

The text opens with the phrase, "Entre la source." By expanding the various denotations of "source"—spring, light, origin—the entire work grows out of it. But at the same time, the word is generating new signifiers which have their *source,* precisely, in the graphemes which compose it: "par*cou*ru," "*trouv*é," "*touch*ant," "*courb*e," the thrice repeated "où," "Touaregs," "tout," "tournoiement," etc. When the work ends, Breton hardly needs to add that this source is "le miroir de mes mots." It would be difficult to find a more effective signifier with which to express both a point of departure and a destination[41] for one's words, one's writing.

Still another type of intertextual repetition concerns a lexeme's capacity to signify earlier literary genres. The "Sonnet" section of Rimbaud's poem, "Jeunesse," is a good illustration of this kind of repetition, even though its title is probably *too* perfect a copy. By this I mean that most readers do not have to make any special effort to figure out that Rimbaud's text is playing with the signification of the term, "sonnet." The title informs us immediately that on some level the work is trying to copy that fixed form. In order to isolate two functions of the signifier "sonnet," we therefore have to settle for the relatively uninteresting pair, sonnet and *non*-sonnet. After all, a modicum of literary competence is required to see that the poem in actuality is not a sonnet. As Roger Little demonstrates in his exacting study of the poem's prosody: "There is a discreet and purposely evasive organization of the 'sonnet' aimed at disturbing self-satisfied response patterns [of the reader] . . ."[42]

On the other hand, "Antique" in the *Illuminations* presents itself in a manner that demands more literary competence on the part of the reader:

Antique

Gracieux fils de Pan! Autour de ton front couronné
de fleurettes et de baies, tes yeux, des boules pré-
cieuses, remuent. Tachées de lies brunes, tes joues se
creusent. Tes crocs luisent. Ta poitrine ressemble à
une cithare, des tintements circulent dans tes bras
blonds. Ton coeur bat dans ce ventre où dort le double
sexe. Promène-toi, la nuit, en mouvant doucement cette
cuisse, cette seconde cuisse et cette jambe de gauche.

Because this text demands more literary competence than certain others do, it helps advance a bit further the case for active participation in the reading act. Indeed, what the signifier "Antique" can refer to is both the dictionary definitions of that word *and* the parnassian poetry in Leconte de Lisle's *Poèmes Antiques*. For verification of this intuition, I shall compare Rimbaud's text with Leconte de Lisle's "Pan."[43]

Beforehand, I should point out that, contrary to Leconte de Lisle, Rimbaud talks about the "Gracieux fils de Pan," and not Pan himself. Since Pan was the god of fertility, or more specifically, of all nature, this son could theoretically represent anyone or anything whatsoever. While most critics have noted this difference, none of them seems to lend any great importance to it. Following his friend Delahaye's suggestion that Rimbaud probably saw an ancient statue in a park one night, they go on to read the subsequent details in the context of this purported referent.[44] Owing to the immobility of Pan's son in the description, one understands their persistence in keeping so attractive an hypothesis. The presence of satyr-like fangs merely reinforces that assumption.

Compared to the parnassian version of Pan, however, Rimbaud's creature appears rather anomalous. A closer look at Leconte de Lisle's Pan reveals a similar ordering of details, but ultimately, a much different description. Although both texts begin commenting on the forehead, for instance, Rimbaud's personage is "couronné de fleurettes et de baies." Leconte de Lisle's Pan is "armé de deux cornes" and "bruyant," not "gracieux," like his imagined son. The stock "pieds de chèvres" of fauns and satyrs, mentioned in the first line of the verse, do not figure in the prose poem at all. They are instead replaced by thighs and legs, bodily parts that are restricted neither to humans nor to human-like animals.

There are other differences too. Pan is often portrayed playing a syrinx or a lyre. At the same time, he embodies a kind of lusty, vigorous, athletic exuberance. It should not be possible to affirm, as Rimbaud does, that "[sa] poitrine ressemble à une cithare," and that "[ses] joues se creusent."[45] But since the text does say those things, we are forced to conclude that Pan's son is much less healthy than his father. His face is drawn and his ribs are showing. As a matter of fact, considering his "double sexe," this creature resembles Pan's brother Hermaphroditus much more than would any supposed son of his.[46] Is Rimbaud confused about whom he is trying to describe?

The final bizarre trait of this prose poem is that it avoids the nymph-chasing scene so typical of other *Poèmes Antiques* or Mallarmé's "L'après-midi d'un faune," to cite one of countless other eclogues. Rather than race around at night half-crazed, Pan's *son* is told, "Promène-toi, la nuit, en mouvant doucement cette cuisse, cette seconde cuisse et cette jambe de gauche." This painfully slow movement turns Pan's furious nocturnal romp into a ridiculous leisurely stroll. It stands in marked opposition to the following action in Leconte de Lisle's poem:

> Pan, d'amour enflammé, dans les bois familiers
> Poursuit la vierge errante à l'ombre des halliers,
> La saisit au passage; et, transporté de joie,
> Aux clartés de la lune, il emporte sa proie.

Remembering the first distinction we observed, anyone *vs.* Pan, we now comprehend that Rimbaud's "Antique" functions as a verseless,[47] misshapen, character-deflating copy of the classical mythological portrait of Pan. Instead of there being extensive textual contours (as in the case of "Les bons chiens") to tip off the reader, it is the single word "Antique" that provides the structural matrix for this particular prose poem. By mixing antique code with (anti) Parnassian form, Rimbaud produces a unique "poème antique."

Our categorization of formal intertextual phenomena would not be complete if we did not at least mention the one prose poem in which a single letter—not word—repeats several anterior models. Because Rimbaud's "H" sets into motion a linguistic unity that (potentially) re-presents every word beginning with an "h," the reader is able to interpret the work in as many ways as there are such words.

H

Toutes les monstruosités violent les gestes atroces d'Hortense. Sa solitude est la mécanique érotique, sa lassitude, la dynamique amoureuse. Sous la surveillance d'une enfance elle a été, à des époques nombreuses, l'ardente hygiène des races. Sa porte est ouverte à la misère. Là, la moralité des êtres actuels se décorpore en sa passion ou en son action—O terrible frisson des amours novices sur le sol sanglant et par l'hydrogène clarteux! trouvez Hortense.

When asked to explain the poeticity of this text, critics will insist that "H" *means* Hortense or hygiene or hydrogen. That is, it is "about" one of those text-based words. Given the pronunciation [aʃ] and other lexical recollections occasioned by the letter, they may otheɪwise point out its connection to hashish or masturbation.[48]

What all these interpretations suggest is that the text does not really mean anything at all. Or rather, they make it evident that all those things are meant, along with, very probably, many more. This is tantamount to saying that the signifier "H," thanks to its peculiar form, repeats each element of the sociolect which the individual reader recalls when he perceives it. In that sense, it is actually an exemplary intertextual copy. It illustrates the very process by which one text signifies in relation to other texts.

Are we then condemned to repetition by our use of the alphabet in general? At the risk of making repetition appear either trivial or silly, I have to answer in the affirmative. Because the alphabet is finite, then any iterative series in a text, especially an alliterative series, will tempt the writer to emulate the established pattern, and to restrict thereby the choice of words available to him. For the reader/interpreter as well, repeated letters and their corresponding phonemes tend to create a kind of phonostylistic dimension which they often mistakenly relate back to random words, ideas, or images that begin with, or at least, contain those same letters. A reiterated [s], for instance, will recall to some readers the word *snake*, and thus induce them to see in the text a subliminal diabolical presence. This interpretive strategy works convincingly only when the deduced model (snake) actually appears in the work, or functions as a presupposition of something in the work.[49] Claiming that this particular signified pertains to *any* random context on the sole basis of a repeated [s], therefore, does not hold water, inasmuch as hundreds of other words use the same letter. Any such semantic deduction must be made in view of the other signifiers on the page; it cannot be justified universally and outside of a specific context.

Now when Robert Greer Cohn asserts that "H" is "not poetry, of course, but a sort of veiled confession, hence barely literary,"[50] one gets an excellent idea of how criticism frequently substitutes biography for linguistic intertextuality. It is not necessary to know about Rimbaud's tumultuous life in order to realize that this is a literary text. It suffices to note the debt it has to a model (the letter "h") outside the margins that define it, and to demonstrate how its "inside" copies this preexisting element into a new form.

From this point of view, "H" can be considered a hymn (another "h") to the literary possibilities of graphemes themselves.[51] Unlike any other letter in French, /h/ functions as a purely graphemic mark, an unpronounced[52] mark that does not *stand for* any sound whatsoever. This implies that it is not a sign at all, but merely a visual trace of an historical stage in the development and standardization of written French. No other letter could better illustrate the unbridgeable gap between the written and the conceptual. At the same time, no other could better underscore the ineluctability of intertextual repetition within a closed linguistic system; here, the alphabet.

So while finding "H" is the critical goal of this game, seeking her (it?) out is its real conclusion, "trouvez Hortense." To delve into the linguistic heritage of this text is exactly equivalent to leaving it. The literariness of this prose poem, just like that of the other texts we have analyzed so far, thus lies to a large extent in the search for what it is *not*. Presently, we need to develop a more precise description of what this type of literature, in all its materiality, *is*.

NOTES

[1] For this reason, their study logically precedes that of *intra*textual repetitions. If we are to arrive at a minimal classification of semiotically charged linguistic models, it makes sense for us to begin with those which are already accepted as such.

[2] Culler, "Literary Competence," p. 103.

[3] Obviously, the more literary competence a reader has, the more likely it is that he ascertain a text's genre before finishing it.

[4] That is, the stylistic dimension of a text defined and delimited by its intertextual repetitions.

[5] And even though they differ from these external paradigms in specific instances, the paradigms or models are still the only linguistic entities that can be *named* and, hence, used by the critic. Therein lies their analytical pertinence.

[6] Shlomith Rimon-Kenon, "Paradoxical status of repetition," *Poetics Today*, 1, No. 4 (1979), 153.

[7] "Paradoxical status of repetition," p. 153.

[8] In the light of the lexical intertextual repetitions outlined later in this chapter, I wonder whether there was a subliminal pun in the mind of Baudelaire on the latin *cano* (I sing) and *canum* (dog) behind his choice of dogs. Lacking more textual evidence, I can only speculate as to Baudelaire's intention.

[9] In Ronsard's ode "A luy-mesme" in Pierre Ronsard, *Oeuvres complètes*, ed. Gustave Cohen (Paris: Bibliothèque de la Pléiade, 1950), p. 368.

[10] As in Keats' "Ode to a Nightingale."

[11] The three parts of a regular Pindaric ode should be of equal length, and have a similar versification system.

[12] This notion is explained further in Riffaterre, *Semiotics of Poetry*, pp. 63-70.

[13] As will Rimbaud in his "Vénus Anadyomène." See Riffaterre, *La Production du texte*, pp. 93-97.

[14] On one level, all words are. They all copy something from somewhere else because otherwise they would not mean anything to anyone. Words in a literary text, however, often signify several ways *at the same time*, unlike those in "ordinary" writing. Since the majority of Rimbaud's titles have only one word, they frequently work as lexical copies for two or more "referents." For more on this, see the third part of this chapter, pp.57-65

[15] Examples of previous speculation are in Rimbaud, *Oeuvres*, ed. Bernard, p. 534.

[16]The Surrealists, of course, were particularly fond of mystery. Breton found this text so intriguing he even set up an altar to Léonie Aubois d'Ashby.

[17]Rimbaud's "Soir Historique" plays the same trick, only with time. Instead of indicating the precise date of this "historic" evening, the prose poem begins: "En quelque soir, par exemple. . . ." This deliberate temporal uncertainty undermines the denotative sense of the adjective "historic." Why does Rimbaud have recourse to such stylistic sleight of hand? I leave the answer to that question to the sociological, psychoanalytic, Marxist, and biographical critics, preferring merely to identify—as is consistent with my proposed aims—the linguistic categories or paradigms with which Rimbaud's style plays.

[18]See appendix for entire text, pp.138-140.

[19]According to Tzvetan Todorov in his *Introduction à la littérature fantastique* (Paris: Seuil, 1970), p. 29, "Le fantastique, c'est l'hésitation éprouvée par un être qui ne connaît que les lois naturelles, face à un événement en apparence surnaturel."

[20]Gérard de Nerval, *Les Filles du Feu* (Paris: Garnier-Flammarion, 1965), pp. 153-77.

[21]Gérard de Nerval, *Oeuvres*, ed. Henri Lemaitre (Paris: Garnier, 1966), I, p. 20.

[22]See Riffaterre's ideas on scrambling in his *Semiotics of Poetry,* pp. 138-50.

[23]Valery, *Oeuvres,* tome I, p. 148.

[24]Barbara Johnson observes a constant shift from metaphor to metonymy throughout Baudelaire's prose poems. See her "Quelques conséquences de la différence anatomique des textes," *Poétique,* 28 (1976), 455.

[25]Hugo, *Notre-Dame de Paris* (Paris: Garnier-Flammarion, 1967), p. 140.

[26]Barbara Johnson interprets this text as an illustration of how a prose poem breaks the fixed versification of a proper poetic verse. She bases her analysis in part on reading the syntagm *casser les verres* as a pun on the words *verres/vers*. Her interpretation lends support to my point concerning the category of phrasal intertextuality I am developing here. See her discussion in *The Critical Difference,* p. 45.

[27]This sociolectic recollection is inevitable because, as the dictionary indicates, the word *déluge* most frequently occurs in expressions like "remonter au Déluge" or "*avant* le Déluge." The primary usage of it with the adverb "after" is the one we find in our deduced model, "Après moi, le Déluge!"

[28]Cf. Albert Py's remark in his edition of *Illuminations* (Genève: Librairie Droz, 1967), p. 85: "L'invocation au nouveau déluge ne trahit pas la nostalgie d'un nihiliste, mais le rêve d'un révolté qui refuse la dimension historique."

[29]This is in effect the circular and iterative situation of epistemology discussed in chapter one.

[30]That exact quotations are not crucial to prose poem functioning (and, indeed, are to be avoided) can be inferred from Baudelaire's "La Solitude." There, the narrator is neither sure of the author, nor of the particular source: " 'Ce grand malheur de ne pouvoir être seul!...' dit quelque part La Bruyère"; and " 'Presque tous nos malheurs nous viennent de n'avoir pas su rester dans notre chambre', dit un autre sage, Pascal, je crois . . ."! This runs completely contrary to the precision of his poetry.

[31]Unlike a case of ambiguity, this syntagm signifies in two ways *simultaneously*. The question is not to figure out which of two senses is meant (ambiguity), but rather to understand *both* in the same instance.

[32]Although a similar usage of it can be found later on in the same piece when the poor family, described in Christian code (as opposed to the rich family they are staring at), is qualified as being a "famille *d'yeux.*"

[33]The *Trésor de la langue française* attests to this syntagm's usage as early as 1859 for the plural form, and 1867 for the singular, both of which precede Rimbaud's text.

[34]This is one of the principles Riffaterre finds in prose poem poetics. See his *Semiotics of Poetry*, pp. 116-17.

[35]Maurice Maeterlinck, *Serres chaudes* (Bruxelles: Lacomblez, 1895), p. 89.

[36]Let us not forget that in his verse-poem, "Le Voyage," the narrator greets old captain Death at a port and decides to *leave* with him. Here again the prose poem plays off an earlier poetic model, repeating it but differing from, and deferring it.

[37]Dumarsais-Fontanier, *Les Tropes* (Genève: Slatkine Reprints, 1967), p. 174. Also see Michael Riffaterre, "La Syllepse intertextuelle," *Poétique*, 4 (1979), 496-501.

[38]For an expanded discussion of this point, see Algirdas Julien Greimas, *Du sens* (Paris: Seuil, 1970), pp. 7-17.

[39]In Rimbaud's "Dévotion," above, pp. 45-47.

[40]Peirce, *Collected Papers*, 1.339.

[41]As in the expression, "remonter *aux* sources."

[42]Quoted from his "Rimbaud's 'Sonnet,' " *Modern Language Review*, 75, Part 3 (July 1980), 533.

[43]Leconte de Lisle, *Oeuvres complètes, Poèmes antiques* (Paris: Librairie Alphonse Lemerre, 1927), pp. 128-29.

[44]Rimbaud, *Oeuvres*, ed. Bernard, p. 488.

[45]To compare his chest to a lyre is to hint at a kind of scrawniness that one associates with undernourishment. Saying that his face is drawn merely intensifies this sense.

[46]Lautréamont paints an extraordinarily similar picture of an hermaphrodite in *Les Chants de Maldoror.* See his *Oeuvres complètes* (Paris: Garnier-Flammarion, 1969), pp. 95-98.

[47]With the exception of the sixth line, a perfect alexandrine. This exception is emblematic of the classical poetic norms which the text transcends.

[48]Robert Greer Cohn alludes to several of these readings. See his *The Poetry of Rimbaud* (Princeton: Princeton University Press, 1973), p. 380.

[49]See my section on paragrammatic repetitions in chapter three for more on this point, pp. 85ff. The strategy I am talking about here derives from a consideration of *intra*textual, more than *inter*textual repetition.

[50]Cohn, *The Poetry of Rimbaud*, p. 380.

[51]Cf. Jean-Louis Baudry's remark, "toute réponse qui a pour but de substituer un signifié au texte écrit 'H' ne peut être que partielle et inadéquate au texte lui-même, et ne se présentera que comme un signifiant supplémentaire, signifiant de lecture qui se joue du lecteur." See his "Le Texte de Rimbaud" (fin), *Tel Quel*, 36 (1969), 46.

[52]Obviously, one pronounces the /h/ when reciting the alphabet, but never when reading it in conjunction with other letters in a word or phrase.

Chapter III

INTRATEXTUAL REPETITIONS

> . . . le signe échappe toujours en une
> certaine mesure à la volonté individuelle
> ou sociale, c'est là son caractère essentiel;
> mais c'est celui qui apparaît le moins à
> première vue.[1]
>
> --Saussure

If a text owes much of its poeticity to certain preestablished sign systems, it is no less true that its actual formal makeup constitutes a wholly unique combination of signs. Borrowing Deleuze's term, we can say that every literary work, by virtue of this very specificity, is an *apprésentation*. Being both re-presentation and presentation, it has "no present" to speak of at all, except as it relates figuratively to the moment when poetic features are noted during the reading-act. A text's historical present or coming into being, in other words, is but one moment in the existence it has for actual readers. What it refers back to and what it produces (by way of "new" models) are far more significant dimensions of its literariness. Therefore, since a writer writes his work a certain way and not another, one should not compare it exclusively to other texts. While it does re-present features identifiable *at some point* in the reading-act with a myriad of intertextual models, a text presents other features that must first be reckoned with in terms of their apparently absolute difference from anything else a reader has ever seen.

But as indicated earlier in our theoretical preliminaries, any explanation or articulation of difference points to the *possibility of finding a repetition*. To insist that a given work, or even part of a work, both differs from and defers other works is to beg the question of what these "others" are. In our last section we observed various intertextual models, i.e., "others," which particular works came to alter. Here, it will be necessary to explore more closely the manner in which a literary text, with each new linguistic element it puts into play, signifies *differently* from itself, i.e., from its other component parts. In the light of repetition's paradoxical nature this description of a text's operation suggests that literary works really express the same thing(s) over and over again. So one has to determine whether iterative relationships found within the work do in fact produce dissimilar messages, or whether they merely repeat the same one.

What is there about a context that permits the reader to comprehend a point he thinks a text is "trying" to make? Part of the answer lies in its capacity to refer us to *external* models, as has already been shown. Failing this capacity, a text cannot communicate with us at all, since it would not fall into the realm of the already-known, the area of our language memory. When a reader articulates nothing of what he is reminded of, either to himself or to a public, the text simply passes right through him. In a sense, it goes in one eye and out the other.

Within academic or professional circles this situation is, of course, quite rare. With very few exceptions,[2] critics are wont to talk about, analyze, and comment on a work beyond just experiencing it. Even so, though commentary and interpretation are central to almost any critical enterprise, the critic who concludes anything whatsoever about a poem will perforce rely on models, be they sociological, psychological, linguistic, and the like. From this perspective, the interaction between a textual feature and a specific model or reference point produces hermeneutic remarks themselves.

When a text—thanks to a repetition—induces us to return to a different point within its own margins *before* reminding us of something we already know, our reading is grounded on *internal* rather than external models. If this distinction appears artificial, it at least accounts for the empirical fact that with each re-reading, or new study, a different set of textual criteria is chosen for examination. Be that as it may, the perceived copying of internal models is what defines intratextual repetition. The largest reading space in which one observes such repetitions is the sentence. Anything above that threshold necessarily overlaps onto the *inter*textual domain. The reason for this is that when longer, semiotically marked units (strophes, dialogue, etc.) are repeated, the experienced reader recognizes previous genres or discourses that the text copies intertextually.

This limit notwithstanding, an analyst's description includes instances when a phrase has to be related to another one within that same text before being linked later on to an intertextual model. Prior to its "communicating," that is, a repetitive signal of this type must first be noted by the reader. This phenomenon, frequently encountered in the reading act, will be named *phrasal intratextual repetition*. By drawing the reader's attention to another sentence or sentence fragment from that same text, this kind of repetition brings into focus a sometimes neglected equivalency on which the work depends in order to transmit certain bits of supplementary information. Like the other stylistic features discussed in this chapter, this one too can function with respect to, or in spite of, an author's volition and intention.

Phrasal Repetitions

To illustrate this aspect of literariness, I shall begin with an analysis of one of Baudelaire's better-known prose poems:

LE MIROIR

Un homme épouvantable entre et se regarde dans la glace.
"—Pourquoi vous regardez-vous au miroir, puisque vous ne pouvez vous y voir qu'avec déplaisir?"
L'homme épouvantable me répond: "—Monsieur, d'après les immortels principes de 89, tous les hommes sont égaux en droits; je possède le droit de me mirer, avec plaisir ou déplaisir, cela ne regarde que ma conscience."
Au nom du bon sens, j'avais sans doute raison; mais, au point de vue de la loi, il n'avait pas tort.

The setting of the poem seems fairly straightforward: a homely man comes in and looks at himself in a mirror. The question arises, presumably from the narrator, as to why he bothers putting himself through such an unpleasant ordeal. The latter points out that in regard to the immortal principles of 1789 he has a perfect right to look at himself, regardless of any displeasure he may experience in the process. The act of considering his mirror-image, says the man, "ne regarde que ma conscience."

Forced to accept this unusual rationale, the somewhat flustered narrator promptly admits: "Au nom du bon sens, j'avais sans doute raison; mais, au point de vue de la loi, il n'avait pas tort." With this the text abruptly ends. While a reader pondering Baudelaire's laconic conclusion may very well be content with its patness, he will most probably also notice the symmetry or repetitiveness of the two sentences which form it. But when he attempts to show just how the two are related, an additional formal feature comes to light. Made up of a subordinate clause beginning with *Au*, and an independent clause, the first line sets up a pattern which the second line initially copies. What also happens formally is that *nom* turns into *point de vue, bon sens* into *loi, je* into *il,* and *raison* into *tort.* Given their equivalent positions, these lexical changes reinforce the radical philosophical and existential separation which the text establishes between the *homme épouvantable* and the narrator. *Je,* in other words, appears to want to distinguish himself from the *il* whom he is observing.

Yet to say that one person was no doubt right, and that the other was not wrong is to assert essentially nothing. Though it takes the guise of a conclusion, the couplet does not resolve the matter of who is right and who is wrong in the least. On the contrary, the reader is left with the impression that both individuals are correct in their respective points of view. If I may be permitted a bit of word play, the repetitive sequence implies that having rights is not the same as being in the right.

My choice of the term "couplet" in the last paragraph is not gratuitous. By using it I intended to emphasize the versified nature of this phrasal intratextual repetition. Indeed, the model line in "Le Miroir" (the first in the couplet) can be read as an alexandrine: it contains twelve syllables in the 5-7 order with the caesura after the words *bon sens*. The copy line, on the other hand, reverses this metric order to 7-5 with a break after *loi*. Inasmuch as the word *mais* forms an extra syllable in this hypothesized verse environment, it is of course inconsistent. Considering the uncertainty[3] among editors vis-à-vis its typographical position, it might then be read as a kind of enjambment. By subverting the twelve-syllable requirement of alexandrines, the extra syllable would bring it that much more into relief, and to our attention. This problem, to be sure, may not arise at all in either prose or poetry. Yet in prose poems, editors determine to a great extent the impact a given line has on its readers.

Having shown that the couplet provides only the semblance of a conclusion, we can now undertake an evaluation of its peculiar formal structure. Is it pertinent to the poem or not? While opposing *je* to *il*, the two lines—we have said—repeat the same syntactic pattern. Simultaneous to that repetition, though, is what amounts literally to a *mirroring* of the first (5-7) by the second (7-5). In retrospect, this secondary effect creates confusion as to the true identities of the two characters. Provided we have read the text carefully, this formal aspect obliges us to re-think the problem of who is who in this piece. Aware of the similarity between the mirror-like rhythm of the conclusion and the prose poem's title itself, the reader should now reappraise one of his very first assumptions. Was he too hasty in believing there were two separate characters in the text?

Backtracking to a cause for the observed specular effect makes us want to reread the introduction:

> Un homme épouvantable entre et se regarde dans la glace.
> "—Pourquoi vous regardez-vous au miroir, puisque vous ne pouvez vous y voir qu'avec déplaisir?
> L'homme épouvantable me répond: "—Monsieur . . . cela ne regarde que ma conscience."

Who is this man and who poses him this question? Our initial reaction—based on the indirect pronoun "me"—was that a narrator asked a hideous man why he bothers looking at himself. Considering the absence of any further precisions, could it be that our assumed narrator exists, not independently of the man, but rather as his mirror image? Although the expression, "ça ne regarde que . . ." is, as they say, a mere manner of speaking, it would appear particularly appropriate here for two reasons. First, the man's response, "cela ne regarde que ma conscience," repeats the verb from the reflexive form *se regarde* which described that same man's action in the opening scene. Secondly, were we to replace the demonstrative pronoun *cela* with the words it stands for, the phrase would read something like this: "le fait de me regarder ne regarde que ma conscience."

What all of this means is that mirrors and mirror-images abound in this prose poem, though perhaps none so important formally as the phrasal repetition at the end. Itself shaped as a metric mirror-image, the sentence pair restates the text's whole problematic concerning mirrors. From the question of who is talking in the poem, one moves on to the more pressing questions of who is ugly, and in what way.[4] After all, in order for an individual to be thought of as ugly, it requires that he be seen by someone, and that someone be conscious of his ugliness. Yet pangs of conscience traditionally foster an awareness of one's own metaphorical ugliness, the blemished image of one's inner self à la Dorian Gray or Mr. Hyde. Might it be that Baudelaire is fantasizing about his ugly other self from the point of view of this other?

Concerning mirror-images, the distinction between consciousness of oneself and one's conscience thus remains open to discussion, and literary utilization. This is especially true in French, where *conscience* can signify both states. There would be no problem then in our labeling the word *conscience* a lexical intertextual copy, as we defined in chapter two. Far from excluding one another, the various repetitions outlined in our essay work in relation to each other.

Poisson soluble no. 2, unlike Baudelaire's text, commences with a repetitive sentence pair: "Moins de temps qu'il n'en faut pour le dire, moins de larmes qu'il n'en faut pour mourir: j'ai tout compté, voilà." Comprised of a parallel structure and a short commentary, this model generates an ostensibly obsessional concern for formal parallelism throughout the poem. For every element A the text furnishes an A^1 which, instead of developing out of the first element, however, seems to undermine the very notion of development or "proper" order. It is as if once a parallel is drawn, the scriptor can no longer know, or no longer cares, which textual unity comes first. The parallelism itself takes precedence over what is being paralleled, making it a marvellous illustration of the surrealist game "L'un dans l'autre."[5]

Consider the following excerpts: "je ne sais plus que penser du suicide car, si je veux me séparer de moi-même, la sortie est de ce côté, j'ajoute malicieusement: l'entrée, la rentrée de cet autre côté." Because the author cannot decide whether he is coming or going, the whole question of suicide ends up suspended or, at least, put in parentheses. Next he says: "je suis seul, je regarde par la fenêtre: il ne passe personne ou plutôt personne ne *passe* (je souligne passe)." Since he is alone, one might have expected him to underline *personne* rather than *passe*. Right after this he asks: "Ce

Monsieur, vous ne le connaissez pas? C'est M. Lemême. Je vous présente Madame Madame." While the actual identities of these people are impossible to know, that does not prevent Breton from doubling them up and then associating each to the other with the aid of the terse *Et leurs enfants*.

In view of these aberrant syntagms, the following conclusion about this text can be made. Whenever we as critics try to stress one of the models more than the copy, it is a bit like saying that line A is more "important" than line A^1 in the geometric relationship of parallels. Seeking out the *raison d'être* of a given element in the poem brings to mind the fate of *Je*: "Puis je reviens sur mes pas, mes pas reviennent aussi mais je ne sais pas exactement sur quoi ils reviennent." The reason he does not know "sur quoi ils reviennent" is that his place of origin is totally contingent on an earlier utterance, the earliest being the introductory phrasal repetition. The rest of the scriptual course (*trajet*) involves counting out and making the necessary correspondences between the narrative "steps": "j'ai tout compté, voilà."

That the poem undermines the concept of a correct sequentiality may be inferred from the way the narrator consults a train schedule: "Irai-je à A, retournerai-je à B, changerai-je à X?" In "normal" geometry one would begin at A, go to B, and then possibly return to A. Changing at X is merely a commentary, a putting into perspective of two otherwise arbitrary poles, much as was the syntagm *Et leurs enfants*. What is especially interesting here is that, according to the author, ennui is part and parcel of each correspondence between train lines. Under other circumstances, which is to say, lacking a correspondence, these lines would, of course, not meet: "Oui, naturellement, je changerai à X. Pourvu que je ne manque pas la correspondance avec l'ennui!"

Yet, lines that do not meet are parallel lines, like the parallel structure in the opening repetitive sequence; or, metaphorically, like the unconnected train lines which the correspondence with ennui alone connects: "Nous y sommes: l'ennui, les belles parallèles, ah! que les parallèles sont belles sous la perpendiculaire de Dieu." This final line, the ultimate and exemplary avatar of the text's parallelism, restates the Baudelairean concept of ennui in all its details. The ennui-free paradise of the latter's "La Chambre double," we recall, subsisted only because there was no time: "il n'est plus de minutes, il n'est plus de secondes! Le temps a disparu; c'est l'Eternité qui règne, une éternité de délices!" And if one needed an effective, albeit unconventional metaphor[6] for such blissful infinity, one could get none better than parallel lines. Since there are no lines (literally, *no correspondences)* to connect them, parallel lines stretch out independent of each other forever.

Nevertheless, the most efficient or closest connection one could make between them, if one wanted, is a perpendicular line. Analogous to the "coup terrible, lourd" on his door that brutally interrupts Baudelaire's *countless* hours of bliss, such a line slices through eternally unconnected parallels whose "beauty" is only then realized.[7] It cannot be realized sooner because there is no awareness without differentiation, and no differentiation without some kind of interruption.

If Breton's text ends with a perpendicular in the midst of beautiful parallels, this image is no doubt also overdetermined at that point by the graphemic character of the writing itself. This writing recalls that of an "écriture perpendiculaire," defined as a writing "dont les lignes sont dirigées de bas en haut et de haut en bas" (Larousse). This type of writing describes precisely what happens to the lines or traits in the text's individual graphemes at the mention of the word *l'ennui*! There is the sudden appearance of two exclamation points; there are none in the rest of the text. There is also a remarkable proliferation of the letter /l/ in *belles parallèles*, which is repeated.[8]

All of these formal aspects, hinted at by an initial phrasal repetition, combine to produce a literary text. Although the individual reader eventually reaches "out" of the work and recovers certain intertextual models, e.g., Baudelaire and Lautréamont (which, to him or her, constitute the real "point" of the text), it is incontestable that the model at the beginning puts him on the right track in describing the poeticity of *Poisson soluble* no. 2.

The *Illuminations* are rife with reiterated sentences and fragments. Taken in their entirety, these and other formal repetitions create what Suzanne Bernard calls Rimbaud's *prose rythmique*.[9] Some actual effects of this rhythmic prose on the reader can be more fully appreciated when we examine a few examples for ourselves, beginning with "Enfance."[10] While the relationship of childhood to the first part of the poem is not immediately obvious, the terms *petite morte, jeune maman*, and *petit frère* in section II suggest a decidedly childish choice of vocabulary. However, when we get to repetitions that I can express as *il y a X* and *Je suis X* in sections III and IV respectively, there is no longer any doubt. Knowing that the style of the text is mimetic of children's speech the reader then returns to earlier parts of the text better prepared for his reading.[11] Alert to the idiom at work, an idiom confirmed by a phrasal repetition, he profits from it retroactively. He sees more clearly the possible cognitive processes behind certain linguistic and narrative choices, and how they might effectively "reflect" childhood. The "origin" of the text is not the issue here, but the origin of our understanding of it.

In Rimbaud's "Départ," the series of sentence fragments "Assez vu . . . Assez eu . . . Assez connu . . ." serves much the same purpose:

Assez vu. La vision s'est rencontrée à tous les airs.
Assez eu. Rumeurs des villes, le soir, et au soleil, et toujours.
Assez connu. Les arrêts de la vie.—O Rumeurs et Visions!
Départ dans l'affection et le bruit neufs!

It too obliges us to go backwards; in this case, in order to retrieve the unsaid matrices or "deep structures" for the fragments, "J'en ai assez _____," "On en a assez _____," etc. Because it causes this recollection, some may object that the fragments in the series act more like *inter*textual than *intra*textual copies. On the condition that we recognize this text's particular insistence on the pattern "Assez X" *before* relating it to the title, the objection can be granted. Unlike "Dévotion," for instance, which has an imminent association with the preestablished pattern "à X," the signifier "départ" has no such necessary connection with "Assez X." One could leave because one had to, and not necessarily because one had had enough. The idea of departing might very well be unappealing to the individual.

Being one kind of copy (intertextual) does not therefore prevent a textual unity from being the other kind as well. Once again, the classificatory problem involves questions of an order in reading (although there is *no* choice in the first reading), and the reader himself. Both questions are explored at length in our final chapter. At this time, the important point to grasp is that only through the intratextual repetition of these fragments can we perceive the (intertextual) pertinence of the title: once one has had enough of someone or something, one leaves.

In "Veillées I" the situation is slightly different. Even though the semantico-syntactic fabric of the phrases, "C'est *a* ni *b* ni *c*" repeats intertextually the "intermediateness" that the signifier "vigils" conjures up—a vigil transpires *between* the states sleeping/waking; eating/sleeping; death/burial—their phonemic organization adds to or overdetermines their contextual suitability. Here is the text:

VEILLÉES

C'est le repos éclairé, ni fièvre, ni langueur, sur le lit ou sur le pré.
C'est l'ami ni ardent ni faible. L'ami.
C'est l'aimée ni tourmentante ni tourmentée. L'aimée.
L'air et le monde point cherchés. La vie.
—Etait-ce donc ceci?
—Et le rêve fraîchit.

A repetition of the vocalic scheme in the word "veillées" [eje] is simultaneous to the repetition of syntactical structures. It begins either exactly [e] or closely [ɛ] at the start of each sentence. It is then continued by the [i] in the words "ni . . . ni," and ends with the last syllable of one line or the first syllable of the next. This shifting back and forth of vowels [e-i-e] within similar phrasal structures re-presents a vigil's aforementioned presupposition of two states. Working alongside the dictionary meanings, or what we might more properly dub the "intertextual heritage" of the signifier *veillées,* the phrasal repetition's formal characteristics thus contribute to this prose poem's[12] communicative potential; and, *a fortiori,* to its poeticity. They signify *vigils* a second time.

These last remarks bring us to a crucial juncture in our discussion. One might like to know in what sense a supplementary formal feature works alongside a signified's intertextual heritage to communicate something more. Put simply, such poetic features operate *paragrammatically*;[13] that is, they act beside the lines in which they are discovered. They do not replace or have priority over the more easily traceable sociolectic components of a given signified. They merely expand and give depth to it. A recent critic offers this explanation of the matter: "The 'surface' of a text may be said to hover over boiling depths, within which a multiplicity of competing messages—at various levels of verbal information—jostle for epiphany."[14] So the more we examine finer, less visible idiosyncracies of a text, the further we plunge into its "boiling depths." The advantage of our typology consists precisely in its re-defining these "competing messages" in terms of the reiterated forms they don.

Lexical Repetitions

Having sketched out the category of recurrent sentences and fragments, we can now turn our attention to the tiniest unities of prose poems: words and their individual parts. Although the value of "imperfect" word copies will shortly be demonstrated, a study of *lexical intratextual repetition* must begin with the case of exact duplication of words. What additional information of benefit or interest to the reader is carried by formal features of this type? It is the information derived from their deictic function. By this I mean they indicate where a text's signifying chains (formal and semantic) intersect. These are the "nodal points,"[15] which the reader then has the responsibility to reconsider and reevaluate. In this sense, they are similar to italicized words, though not always so obvious.

Whenever someone observes a repetition of a given word or its pronominal equivalent he starts constructing mentally a kind of fundamental architecture of the text. This "architecture" is more or less synonymous with a supposed signified that slowly develops in the reader's mind. Without such a basic textual feature, the *récit* is often devoid of any continuity and communicative potential. It will be rejected by most people for being improbable ("invraisemblable") and/or non-sensical. Kristéva concludes that repetition permits "le vraisemblable" to happen "lorsque chaque séquence peut être dérivée d'une autre dans les cadres de la structure sujet-prédicat (de la motivation et de la linéarisation).[16]

If her conclusion is true, then each occurrence of a word is related to its initial mention as the "predicate," i.e., its expansion and qualification. With every new appearance, something new is added, something that varies according to both the word and the text. In literature, therefore, "l'unité répétée, n'est plus la même, de sorte qu'on peut soutenir qu'une fois répétée, elle est déjà une autre."[17] By differentiating themselves from their models, repeated words or parts of words constitute the most elementary objects of study for the literary analyst. Since they bring a model into relief, they make us read it more carefully. They make us interrogate its identity,[18] its form, and "meaning" a bit longer.

In Baudelaire's prose poem, "Un hemisphère dans une chevelure," for example, the words *cheveux* and *chevelure* constantly reappear. Rather than intertwine several metaphors which transform hair into a fleece, a dark ocean, etc., as Baudelaire's verse poem "La Chevelure" does, this term repeats the same two lexemes over and over again. The upshot is a subordination of all the details evoked by the hair to the hair itself. Whereas the poem tended to confound the *there and then* of *toison, La langoureuse Asie et la brûlante Afrique* and the rest, the prose poem makes explicit its rhetorical combination[19] of the two from the title on: "l'odeur de tes cheveux . . . l'océan de ta chevelure . . . les caresses de ta chevelure . . . l'ardent foyer de ta chevelure . . ."

The consequences of this stylistic trait are significant. If a repetition of the two words shifts the narrative focus from that to which the object (hair) is compared to the object itself, in the process it undermines the very possibility of metaphor. For in indicating the purely rhetorical link between what the narrator is reminded of (vehicle) and the catalyst for these memories (tenor), the prose poem eliminates metaphor's greatest quality: its lyrical or "inspirational" power to fuse normally separate realities. In addition, it calls into question the very identities of these two poles. What was lyrical and "poetic" in the verse, i.e., everything that was *not* the hair, assumes in the prose a secondary almost "*un*-poetic"[20] role in relation to the hair. The prose poem thus exposes the artificiality of the verse-poem's metaphoric relationship between hair's materiality and certain lyric qualities, and transforms those verse elements repeated by the prose, the ocean, the ardent foyer, etc., into elements "somehow foreign to themselves."[21] Because it is presumably "about" hair, the prose is structured around an actual recurrence of that term, not metaphorical substitutes for it. The resulting effect of this is a re-valorization and de-poetization of the hair, a renewed stress on that object which the verse poem never ceases to slide away from.

Lexical repetition in "La soupe et les nauges," another piece from *Le Spleen de Paris*, performs a similar deictic role by drawing our eyes to the endearing epithet *bien-aimée*, applied to the narrator's woman. The text reads as follows:

> Ma petite folle bien-aimée me donnait à dîner, et par la fenêtre ouverte de la salle à manger je contemplais les mouvantes architectures que Dieu fait avec les vapeurs, les merveilleuses constructions de l'impalpable. Et je me disais, à travers ma contemplation: "—Toutes ces fantasmagories sont presque aussi belles que les yeux de ma belle bien-aimée, la petite folle monstrueuse aux yeux verts."
>
> Et tout à coup je reçus un violent coup de poing dans le dos, et j'entendis une voix rauque et charmante, une voix hystérique et comme enrouée par l'eau-de-vie, la voix de ma chère petite bien-aimée, qui disait: "—Allez-vous bientôt manger votre soupe, s. . . b. . . de marchand de nuages?"

The first time we encounter the woman she is described as a *petite folle bien-aimée*, who gives the narrator plenty of food to eat. While sitting at the table the narrator commences a reverie that elevates him to the clouds, and lets him contemplate God's wonderful impalpable creations: "Toutes ces fantasmagories sont presque aussi belles que les yeux de ma belle bien-aimée, la petite folle monstrueuse aux yeux verts." Suddenly he receives a blow on the back from his woman, now described as his "chère petite bien-aimée." Her voice, "hystérique et comme enrouée par l'eau-de-vie," cries out, "—Allez-vous bientôt manger votre soupe, s. . . b. . . de marchand de nuages?"

On this threatening note the text ends, but not without repeating the paradigm (*endearing*) *epithet*, with the copy "s. . . b. . .". The reason for my parentheses is that the term the woman uses for her man hardly qualifies her as endearing or affectionate. In the original, Baudelaire wrote out the words "sacré bougre" instead of disguising them by way of suspension points. Of course, that historical fact is superfluous for anyone who has taken into account the repetition of "bien-aimée" in the suddenly menacing, aggressive context of the prose poem. For it can be deduced from the context. With every mention of that epithet come hints that the man is not terribly well treated at home. When his woman finally turns violent, for instance, "folle" disappears completely from the description we have of her. This makes it seem as if she had heard, or at least suspected, the two earlier occurrences of this adjective, and that the man/narrator is afraid even to write it any more. It is as if the man's contemplation were shared by the woman and that this were not the first such incident.

But the day-dreaming, cloud-contemplating narrator of the beginning, who loved his woman, and yet still thought of her as a "folle monstrueuse" continues to mix his idealizing (*nuages*) with reality (*soupe*). He describes her voice as *rauque et charmante*. When she disrupts his fantasy, however, she becomes simply his "chère petite bien-aimée," for whom we can well imagine his snapping to attention. Indeed, the more he repeats the word "my beloved" the less we believe in his love. We immediately recall the stereotype of innumerable other "henpecked" husbands whose only reply to their wives is "Yes, dear . . ." Directed in our reading by a lexical repetition, therefore, we seek to understand more of the possible significance, intentionality, irony, etc., of the term "bien-aimée."

Poisson soluble no. 9 unfolds as a series of repeated lexemes whose concatenation generates still further repetitions. In the opening line, the narrative voice apostrophizes the night, then rapidly digresses to another object, strings:

> Sale nuit, nuit de fleurs, nuit de râles, nuit capiteuse, nuit sourde
> dont la main est un cerf-volant abject retenu par des fils de tous
> côtés, des fils noirs, des fils honteux.

The strings have taken over center stage from the night. Likewise, every word appearing in the text seems to take precedence over the one that comes right before it. Each new unity (usually a word, but also longer ones like subordinate clauses, questions, and the like) leads, in its turn, to a new repetition:

> Et toi, *bandit, bandit*, ah tu me tues, *bandit* de l'*eau* qui
> effeuilles tes cout*eaux* dans mes yeux, tu n'as donc pitié de rien,
> *eau* rayonnante, *eau* lustrale que je chéris. (my emphasis)

The function of the narrative voice is to address a bandit, who is then qualified as a "bandit of the water who . . ." Abruptly, as if there were nothing unusual in it, the scriptor switches addressees, and opts for the water. This displacement of interest from one object to another (which, in fact, modifies the first), typifies the surrealist exploitation of *la métaphore filée*.[22]

So, what starts off as an apostrophe to one thing ends up as an apostrophe to another.[23] Since duplication of a given lexeme in literature amounts to its alteration, as Kristéva noted, we infer that a lexical copy, just like any other kind, is both a return to *and* a turning-away-from a model. Breton's text thereby takes the shape of a kind of apostrophe for its own sake.

There is, of course, a great paradox here. While the lexical repetitions lure the reader back to evaluate certain words, their true deictic function is to turn him *away* from these words to what they produce. Hence, the first words (*bandit*) are no more "important" than what they give rise to. The notions of a fixed subject, predicate, object or addressee of an apostrophe, and referent, are all completely subverted by the language of the text. They are replaced by a dynamic structure whose formal characteristics and relationships it is the reader's job to elucidate.

If under the rubric "intratextual" we can place copies that repeat models from elsewhere in the same author's corpus, then lexical repetitions have the potential to point out one final aspect of a text's poeticity: its dependence on other products of its author's pen. The mere existence of concordances attests to the reliance of literary critics on this type of formal feature for their professional work. Yet beyond their obvious utility to a psycho-critical analysis à la Mauron of a writer's past, his traumas and obsessions, such statistical tools also help us pinpoint the specific lexicon of that writer. Their evidence tempts us to speak of Hugolian "imagery," Baudelairean "vocabulary," Rimbaldian "style," and the like. Whether we *should* speak in those terms does not concern us here.[24]

Seeing that words belong in the public domain, however, it is absolutely unjustifiable to make them the exclusive property of certain poets alone. To do so is to cling to the simplistic view of author as the stable, unified "I" behind a poem. It is instead more likely that there exist different sorts of personal manners of expression that a given poet, for whatever biographical reasons, decides to utilize. Such *paroles* would not automatically be recognized and shared by other native speakers of his language, precisely because they are idiolectic. They would be brought to the reader's attention by the recurrence of particular words, words that are not necessarily stock labels. By "stock labels" I refer to something like the title of Eluard's poem "Toilette." The reading Riffaterre does of this text[25] shows how important it is to read it in accordance with the conventions of the genre *toilette*, represented by the title. Although I would agree with his conclusions, the great value of his analysis (from my methodological perspective) lies in how it illustrates the power of discursive *inter*textual repetition in the reading act. Rimbaud's "Antique" demonstrates this same power.

But what about an individual, *intra*textual genre, one whose labels are not operative across auctorial boundaries? It is clear, for example, from the number of studies devoted to them that many readers group Rimbaud's "Ville" texts together whenever they attempt to study a single one. And why is this? For the simple reason that that word—or a reasonable facsimile like "Villes," "Métropolitian"—is repeated. That their actual subject matter justifies the grouping is usually inferred from the start.

In analogous fashion, the simple repetition of a word in Baudelaire's verse and prose versions of "Le Crépuscule du soir," "L'Invitation au voyage," and "L'Horloge," or, say, in Paul Valéry's "Féerie" and "Même Féerie," or in countless other literary examples, tends to guide the reader, rightly or wrongly, towards very specific conclusions about textual structures. Regardless of the absolute validity—or lack thereof—of this approach, it is empirically true that an author's prose poems *will* be partially understood in conjunction with his other works, on the condition that the reader find at least lexical repetitions.

Before introducing the third and last category of intratextual repetition, *paragrammatic* (what I loosely called "imperfect" lexical repetition), I must mention a marginal formal feature that is observed mainly in automatic texts. Because Riffaterre has already described its functioning in detail, I shall speak of it here only briefly. The feature in question has to do with the word copies which are neither exact duplicates of their models nor their disseminated fragments along a sentence, like those we will presently discuss. Though I could pick my example almost at random from *Poisson soluble*, I choose text no. 14 because it took me so long to figure it out. A delay in the process of decipherment is often an index of the signifier's capacity to fixate our attention more on a signified than on another signifier. Here is the passage:

> Ailleurs dans une cour de ferme probablement, une femme jongle avec plusieurs boules de bleu de lessive, qui brûlent en l'air comme des ongles.

Since fingernails do not burn in the air, something is definitely wrong with this comparison. Yet when one notes the verb *jongle* in the first part of the sentence, the "error" is instantly rectified. Owing to its formal[26] similarity with the former, *ongles* becomes a perfectly acceptable element of the sentence, much as any rhyming word in verse would. That a copy of *jongle* is generated at all should not surprise anyone. Outside of the word *jungle*, which is commonly pronounced differently from the former, *ongle* is the *only* French word that rhymes with it. The "odder" the signifier, therefore, the deeper the impression it seems to make on the short-term memory of surrealist writers at work. As long as a linguistic unity has an infrequently used shape, the reader can expect it to be repeated in an automatic text.

Because we have no need to recover an intertextual model that would either justify or explain it, this type of feature is to a large extent the purest form of intratextual repetition. But this very purity makes of it a relatively uninteresting aspect of a text's poeticity: once discovered, little more can be said about it. At best, it is a sign of what Riffaterre calls the "automatic effect" of surrealist writing.

Paragrammatic Repetitions

Until now the repetition of various-sized segments of prose poems has permitted us to put our finger on several supplemental bits of information they carry. Having explored the gamut of dimensions from the text *in toto* down to its individual words, we must finally address the following question: do the linguistic components of literary works, through an iteration of subtler, sub-lexical elements, signify anything more to a reader than do those of non-literary works? The most legitimate way to respond to this question is to study linguistic traits which comprise words, and see whether their repetition adds something to the more general "meaning" drawn from the reading of a literary text. Instead of summarily dismissing these word components as irrelevant to the "normal" process of reading, it would appear worthwhile—in the light of our other analyses—to undertake at least a preliminary investigation of their semiotic potential. A future study that would treat these and possibly other related features in works outside of our corpus is the eventual goal of such a project. I attempt to begin that study in chapter four of this essay.

I shall proceed as with every other poetic feature we have isolated so far. When a textual unit recalls something else, it will be our task to describe the nature of the model this "something else" brings into focus. Since graphemes, by definition, form the common base of all writings in a given language, we do not have the right to assign just any outside (intertextual) model to a particular graphemic sequence. If we did, a reader could claim that a text was repeating almost any word or group of words whatsoever, provided it contained the proper letters of the alphabet. Given this restriction, my next examples are perforce instances of *intra*textual repetition. Failing an internal model, there would be no good reason to think one model more likely to generate a copy than any other one with similar letters: "Pour qu'il y ait effet de sens ici et qu'il s'impose à tous les lecteurs, il devra y avoir au moins une *répétition* qui donnera aux lettres un statut de groupe exceptionnel dans la phrase. Sans clé de ce genre, les lettres peuvent jouer leur rôle au niveau de la langue mais demeurent totalement invisibles, et donc, non existantes, au niveau du style"[27] (my emphasis).

Under the heading "paragrammatic" I therefore include formal features at work throughout a text which are not as clearly delineated as sentences and words. Our hypothesis is this: any recurrence of single letters, letter clusters with no meaning, morphemes, or accent marks *may* express something supplementary to what is signified by the semanticized structures in which they are, so to speak, embedded. Unless one can trace this supplement back to a model inside the text, however, this hypothesis does not apply. For it is that model alone which both triggers and controls memories from the outside.

Anagrammatic

We begin with the case of a complete word which never really appears where we claim it does because it has been fragmented and spread out along the sentence. Historically known as the "anagram," this poetic feature represents a word deduced from a series of letters whose "correct" arrangement would produce it. When the reader makes a conscious link between these letters and other textual paradigms, the dissimulated word is at once revealed to him. The paradigms to which I allude can be either actual signifiers in the text, or else presuppositions of present signifiers.

Rimbaud's "Ouvriers" furnishes our first anagrammatic repetition of a signifier actually present in the text:

OUVRIERS

O cette chaude matinée de février. Le Sud inopportun vint relever nos souvenirs d'indigents absurdes, notre jeune misère.

Henrika avait une jupe de coton à carreau blanc et brun, qui a dû être portée au siècle dernier, un bonnet à rubans, et un foulard de soie. C'était bien plus triste qu'un deuil. Nous faisions un tour dans la banlieue. Le temps était couvert, et ce vent du Sud excitait toutes les vilaines odeurs des jardins ravagés et des prés desséchés.

Cela ne devait pas fatiguer ma femme au même point que moi. Dans une flache laissée par l'inondation du mois précédent à un sentier assez haut, elle me fit remarquer de très petits poissons.

La ville, avec sa fumée et ses bruits de métiers, nous suivait très loin dans les chemins. O l'autre monde, l'habitation bénie par le ciel et les ombrages! Le sud me rappelait les misérables incidents de mon enfance, mes désespoirs d'été dans cet avare pays où nous ne serons jamais que des orphelins fiancés. Je veux que ce bras durci ne traîne plus *une chère image*.

In reading this prose poem, one rapidly becomes aware of a thematic opposition between north and south. The narrator, feeling a warm southern breeze in the cold of winter, suffers with the knowledge that, once again, he must face his cold, bleak industrial town, *cet avare pays*. In this depressing locale, "avec sa fumée et ses bruits de métiers," the man and his wife Henrika survive as well as they can:

Henrika avait une jupe de coton à carreau blanc et brun, qui a dû être portée au siècle dernier, un bonnet à rubans et un foulard de soie. C'était bien plus triste qu'un deuil.

Regardless of her true nationality, Henrika's name *qua* sign has an unmistakable northern "ring" to it,[28] especially in a context of contrast with the south. Even so, she does not tire in the heat like her husband, who remarks, "Cela ne devait pas fatiguer ma femme au même point que moi." The explanation for this is simple. Although he, too, presumably hails from somewhere in the north (he is not named), the south reminds our working class narrator of misery he experienced in his younger days: "Le sud me rappelait les misérables incidents de mon enfance, mes désespoirs d'été. . . ."

But rather than hold that against it, the narrator seems to idealize, even cherish this other part of the world: "O l'autre monde, l'habitation bénie par le ciel et les ombrages!" Torn between his present condition, which *ce bras durci* represents, and his dream of a blessed land (*une chère image*), he thus incarnates the opposition that the rest of the text sketches out. His life, on this February morning, at least, is presented as a conflict of harsh reality (north) and transitory relief (south). From the opening line, the poem sets up this polarity in terms of the temperature: "O cette *chaude* matinée de février"(my emphasis). In the very same phrase, though, the reader discovers the disseminated presence of this worker in anagrammatic form: $O + u + vrier$, a form which literally encompasses these semantically antithetical words. Not only is February among the coldest months of the year, it is also the one month in French that ends in -*vrier*. This makes it the perfect signifier for that textual slot.

Apart from the question of intention, nothing much changes with regard to the informational value of this feature. The less one conceives of anagrams as intended graphemic dislocations, the closer one gets to understanding them for what they are: additional meaningful signals to the reader, whose observations of *all* forms of iteration gains him access to this relatively unexplored level of signification.[29]

Another instance of this type of repetition is found in *Poisson soluble* no. 3, a text we studied in chapter two. Consider how fantastic a scene is set in that poem: one day a giant wasp is descending the boulevard Richard-Lenoir. One can well understand all the fuss it creates. The reader learns that, "En ce temps-là il n'était question tout autour de la place de la Bastille que d'une énorme guêpe. . . ." Since the whole poem is devoted to exactly this *question*, it is natural that the first paragraph gives us some details about the extraordinary wasp.

Yet while the introductory words of the text tell us about "le petit sphinx moderne," and how it sings loudly and poses enigmas to children, the letters which make up the actual words used by Breton restate the entire scene. Inasmuch as the people in the square are discussing nothing other than this wasp, the passage can be said to imply a kind of equivalence between their talk and the "object" of their talk. In different terms, we can express this situation as *question = guêpe*. That is to say, the question on everybody's mind *is* the wasp. Once this rapprochement is made, a striking formal feature comes to light. The initial phoneme [k], and final phoneme [ɔ̃] of the word *question* are repeated throughout the second sentence. For every [k] the reader finds, a corresponding [ɔ̃] follows, usually quite close by. Moreover, their order in the model is nearly always respected.

Le petit sphinx moderne avait déjà fait pas mal de victimes quand, sortant du café au fronton duquel on a cru bon de faire figurer un canon, quoique la Prison qui s'élevait en ces lieux puisse passer aujourd'hui pour une construction légendaire, je rencontrai la guêpe à la taille de jolie femme qui me demanda son chemin.

In this way the paragraph not only states that everyone is talking about wasps, it also adds its own "voice" to the banter. It reproduces the *question* which the wasp's existence posed to begin with, as if to expose the narrator's own incredulity vis-à-vis the creature of which he is *at the same time* giving us an account.

A second kind of anagram, derived instead from presuppositions of an actual text-based word, can be recovered from Rimbaud's "Vies."[30] Certainly, the term "lives" presupposes many things, though perhaps none as much the preposition "of." In common parlance, it is typical to speak of the lives of individuals, nations, etc. In literature, however, this signifier cannot help but evoke some very famous texts whose titles it repeats: Plutarch's *Parallel Lives*, and especially hagiographic works or lives of saints. Insofar as it has this intimate connection with *writings* about certain people, the term by itself signals the genre "biography" or "autobiography."

As soon as we get past the title, Rimbaud's prose poem immediately corroborates this connection: "O les énormes avenues du pays *saint*, les terrasses du *temple!*" (my emphasis). Keeping in mind this now actualized association with saints, the reader notes a certain nostalgia or looking-backwards on the part of the narrator: "Qu'a-t-on fait du brahmane qui m'expliqua les Proverbes? D'alors, de là-bas, je vois encore même les vieilles! Je me souviens des heures d'argent. . . ." The added mention of red pigeons ("pigeons écarlates") serves to reinforce our sense of the exotic, the far-away, the not-here. Interestingly, the adjective "écarlate" appears in only one other place in Rimbaud's work, his sonnet entitled "Le Mal." This poem describes mockingly a horrible battle during which God falls asleep, rocked by gentle hosannahs. With every mention of the said color, Rimbaud seems to favor religious imagery. This is no doubt due, in part, to its traditional usage for robes of cardinals.

Significantly, the closest morphological analogue to this adjective found elsewhere in Rimbaud's poetry (and, at that, only once) is the word "écarlatine," which he utilizes in "Les Lèvres closes vu à Rome," a piece from *Album Zutique*. There we read the following description:

> Il est à Rome, à la Sixtine,
> Couverte d'emblèmes chrétiens,
> Une cassette *écarlatine*
> Où sèchent des nez fort anciens:
> *Nez d'ascètes de Thébaide*,
> Nez de chanoines du Saint-Graal . . . (my emphasis)

Rimbaud's writing appears to juxtapose the linguistic form "écarlat-" to things saintly, especially ascetic.

When our narrator admits he is "exiled here"—wherever *here* may be—his regrets become obvious. Regardless of why he was exiled, he clearly holds the place from where he came in great esteem: "Je vous indiquerais les richesses inouïes." The way we learn of the exile is through a phrase whose shape hints at something beyond the strict semantic content of its words. Introduced by a dash, the first two words are set in apposition with the subject *je*. The emphasis thus placed on them resembles that of a would-be stressed personal pronoun: "—Exilé ici, j'ai eu une scène où jouer les chefs-d'oeuvres dramatiques de toutes les littératures." In addition, the indeterminateness of locale makes "Exilé ici" that much more notable. Since being in exile implies being anywhere *but* here, one might have expected the shifter "*là*" rather than *ici*. With a first person narrator (*Je*), "here" is, of course, a logical necessity. Even so, that does not take anything away from the enigmatic quality of *alors, là-bas,* and finally *ici.* Indeed, it merely increases it.

Given the earlier signs that pointed to the lives of saints, the phonemes in the words "Exile ici" thus bring to the reading space an additional informational unit. Stressed by their position in the poem, they anagrammatically repeat the core of the name *Alexis.* This saint, whose life is the basis for one of the most celebrated hagiographic texts, could not be more applicable to this context. For despite the disguised form it assumes the "ghost" of St. Alexis is certainly present in the body of the work. According to the legend, he spent his whole life in a kind of spiritual exile; first, in a distant land(*là*), and then, under the very noses of the family and wife he left (*ici*). *La Vie de Saint Alexis*, just like Rimbaud's prose poem, deals with what Robert Sabatier calls, "les regrets du temps passé, ceux qu'on trouvera dans tous les siècles et que l'homme vieillissant ponctue toujours d'un soupir."[31] The medieval text commences with the words,

> Bons fut li siecles al tem ancienour,
> Quer feiz i eret e justice ed amours . . .

The wise narrator of "Vies," who also ponders the "good old days," gives his own sigh of resignation:

> J'observe l'histoire des trésors que vous trouvâtes. Je vois la suite! Ma sagesse est aussi dédaignée que le chaos. Qu'est mon néant, auprès de la stupeur qui vous attend?

Influenced by this first anagrammatic repetition, the reader of graphemic forms will be conditioned for his analysis of the later sections in Rimbaud's poem. Having made the connection between the title and works on or by famous people, he looks for further iterative signals which pertain to this paradigm. Section II unfolds like a riddle, "Je suis. . . ." One wants to know exactly who is speaking. Since the unknown narrator describes himself as a musician, the sounds of his text should be of great interest and help to the reader. Right away, a repetition of the sounds [m] and the pair [ã] and [ɔ̃] is noted.

> Je suis un in*ven*teur bien autre*ment* mérit*ant* que tous ceux qui *m'ont* précédé; un *m*usicien *mê*me, qui ai trouvé quelque chose *com*me la clef de l'*am*our. A présent, gentilho*mm*e d'une *cam*pagne aigre au ciel sobre, j'essaye de *m'ém*ouvoir au souvenir de l'*enf*ance *m*endiant*e.* . . .

On the condition that the reader have sufficient literary competence, he will then recognize certain phrases and words that intertextually repeat others he has seen elsewhere. The copies in question are: *gentilhomme d'une campagne aigre, ma forte tête,* and *mon atroce scepticisme.* Although the actual models for these copies are *different,* all of them originate in Montaigne's *Essais.* Montaigne himself has been described by Lanson and countless others as a *gentilhomme campagnard.* One of his great precepts was that it is more important to have a *tête bien faite* than a *tête pleine.* And if ever there was a sceptic more renowned than Seneca it would have to be Montaigne.[32]

Coupled with these intertextual features, the repetition of the sounds [m], [ɔ̃], and [ã] now becomes highly significant. In retrospect, it is seen to act as the primary formal element of the incipient anagram, *MONTAIGNE.* The intratextual *phrasal* copy ("camp*agne aig*re au ciel sobre"→"l'air sobre de cette *ai*gre comp*agne*") provides the necessary *-aigne* ending.[33] Thanks to these formal repetitions, the anagram imposes itself onto our critical awareness. It is no wonder that Montaigne's name should thus appear in a text that puts into practice *formally* the subject matter of his *Essais.* Let us not forget what Montaigne said, "Je suis moi-même la matière de mon livre." As an anagram in Rimbaud's text, therefore, he could materially become its subject, in both senses of the word.

Poisson soluble no. 7 yields two more anagrams of this type, both of which answer each other. The text begins with an allusion to an unexplained secret:

> Si les placards resplendissants livraient leur secret, nous serions
> à jamais perdus pour nous-mêmes, *chevaliers de cette table de*
> *marbre* blanc à laquelle nous prenons place chaque soir
> (emphasis mine).

Anyone at all familiar with legends of the Middle Ages will recognize in the last clause an intertextual copy of the knights of the *Round Table.* The combination of Arthurian legend and secrets thereby creates a context that we could qualify with the words "medieval secrets."

Given this intertextual backdrop,[34] the reader does not hesitate to draw certain conclusions about the poem. For one thing, the knights, who are somewhere inside a palace, tell us how "coups de foudre bouleversent de temps à autre la splendide argenterie. . . ." Seeing this statement here immediately brings to mind one of the most famous (and secretive) medieval *coups de foudre,* that of Lancelot and Guinevere. When the knights add, "Pendant que nous dormons, la reine . . ." we become even more intent on tracing a parallel between the two stories. Lancelot, we recall, would meet Guinevere at night while everyone else was asleep.

As if to drive home the point, the text then refers to "ces merveilleux cavaliers." Having changed the word "knight" into the bolder form "cavalier," it makes the reader that much more convinced of Lancelot's relevance to the present work. Since Lancelot was raised by a fairy, he could legitimately take on the epithet *le merveilleux*. This is especially true here because later on in the poem we find an instance of just this epithet: "l'ombre du merveilleux que personne n'a jamais vue." Since a fairy brought him up at the bottom of a lake, it is fitting that Breton's text has Lancelot and his companions getting together "quand il est nécessaire, au fond de l'eau."

Yet, had it not been for a supplementary formal aspect, all these details might not have convinced us that the prose poem is really "about" Lancelot and Guinevere. What renders it practically undeniable is the anagram found in the phrase, "Voyez-moi ces merveilleux cavaliers . . . ils *lance*nt *le merveilleux l*asso fait de deux bras de femme." Inferring that the woman in this case is the queen from before, the reader isolates the name of the knight he surmised was there all along. After noting this anagram, he understands the poem's constant reference to secrets, special rooms, doors and corridors. Arthur's wife and his trusted knight needed, of course, to manoeuvre and plan their rendez-vous behind the scenes. There might also be an allusion to the different ways, e.g., the underwater bridge, by which Lancelot could enter the castle in which Guinevere was held prisoner (in Chrétien de Troyes's version).

The last paragraph summarizes this whole reconstructed, veiled narration: "Me voici dans les corridors du palais, tout le monde dort. Le vert de gris et la rouille, est-ce bien la chanson des sirènes?" The pronoun in "est-ce" replaces the plural subject "le vert de gris *et* la rouille." It thereby transforms this last syntagm into an *ad hoc* singular form when, strictly speaking, it is plural. In addition to that, while the siren's song has always been synonymous with danger, it is a danger that comes from falling prey to a form of female temptation. If Lancelot runs the risk of losing his life in pursuit of a woman, then Guinevere's very existence could be thought of as *his* siren's song. The text's idiolectic logic thus equates this song to the queen, or if one prefers, *vert de gris et la rouille = la chanson des sirènes =* Guinevere. By inverting the terms in the first expression,[35] one arrives at the following graphemic sequence: *la rouille et le gris de vert.* From there to the letters *(la reine) Guenièvre* is admittedly a large step to take in and of itself. But it is not so large a step for the previously prepared reader who knows that the more unusual the signifier, e.g., *Guenièvre*, the more likely for it to be the site of scriptural gymnastics in an automatic text. The various accepted spellings of that name are further cause for its employment as a lexical model to be copied.

A final reason to think that Guinevere is somehow related to this particular concatenation of signifiers can be found in the specific[36] scene of Chrétien de Troyes's version where Lancelot, at great risk to them both, tries to get together with the Queen. We recall that the major barrier between them was a *grille de fer* (an iron gate), which at the time became the primary object of the narrative's focus. Not only does this gate sound like *gris de vert*, it also belongs to the same semantic field as verdigris and rust. So nothing could serve as a more dangerous "Siren's song" for Lancelot than the iron gate which Guinevere stands behind, and through which he must attempt to pass.

In order to show the total interdependency between anagrams of absent words and a particular stylistic environment, I shall now cite *Poisson soluble* no. 22 as my last example. Riffaterre's analysis[37] of this text proves quite convincingly that its semantic incompatibilities can be resolved by reference to Hugo's *Les Misérables*. A series of what we have been calling intertextual copies allows the former to recover the earlier work and use it as the interpretant for Breton's poem. As accurate as that reading is, the reader of forms possesses an additional textual key confirming Riffaterre's already significant discovery. By concentrating on the simple *intra*textual repetition of phonemes, one notices a very pertinent feature, the extraordinary recurrence of the sounds [ʒ], [v], [l], and [ã], as in Jean Valjean [ʒãvalʒã]. Although not unusual in the same way that *jongle* or *Guenièvre* was, the phonemic transcription of Jean Valjean's name exhibits a kind of peculiar circularity, going from [ʒ] to [v] back to [ʒ]. These four phonemic units recur at a high frequency in Breton's poem:

Cette femme, *Je l'*ai connue d*a*ns une *v*igne imme*n*se, que*l*ques *j*ours a*v*ant *l*a *v*end*a*nge et *je l'*ai sui*v*ie un soir autour du mur d'un cou*v*ent. *E*lle était *en* gra*n*d deuil et *je* me s*en*tais incapab*l*e de résister à ce nid de corbeaux que m'a*v*ait figuré *l'*ec*l*air de son *v*isage tout à *l'*heure, a*l*ors que *je* tenais derrière *ell*e *l'*asc*en*sion des *v*êtem*en*ts de feuilles rouges d*a*ns *l*esque*l*s brimba*l*aient des grelo*t*s de nuit. D'où *v*enait-*e*lle et que me rappe*l*ait cette *v*igne s'é*l*e*v*a*n*t au c*en*tre d'une *v*il*l*e, à *l'* emp*l*acem*en*t du théâtre, p*en*sais-*je*? . . . Cette femme, qui ress*em*b*l*ait à s'y méprendre à *l'*oiseau qu'on appe*ll*e *v*euve, décri*v*it a*l*ors d*a*ns *l'*air une courbe sp*l*e*n*dide, son *v*oi*l*e traî*n*ant à terre t*a*ndis qu'*e*lle s'é*l*e*v*ait . . .

*V*oy*ant* à que*l* point *l*a patie*n*ce a*ll*ait m'être funeste, *je* me
re*v*isai à *t*e*mp*s pour saisir un coin du *v*oi*l*e sur *l*eque*l j'av*ais mis
*l*e pied et qui me *l*i*v*ra *l'en*sem*bl*e du m*ant*eau. . . .

If the reader puts any stock in the text's phonemic repetitions, he now
has even more reasons to accept Riffaterre's point of view. The latter's
conclusion, in essence, was that Jean Valjean is the central character of this
prose poem, even though he does not actually figure into it. But inasmuch as
the poem's forms *intra*textually re-present the phonemes in Jean Valjean's
name ([ʒ], [v], [l], [ã], the reader's *inter*textual analysis is that much more
convincing. While the latter does not *need* the former, it definitely adds
something to it, a new dimension. Not only is the poem "about" *Les
Misérables*, therefore; in a strictly formal sense, it *is* that story.

One might object that this reading technique could be used to prove
that every poem is likewise "about" Jean Valjean. The easiest and most
effective counter-argument to this I can imagine would consist in examining
a random poem of similar length, and seeing whether, in fact, the objection
should be granted. So as to limit the number of possible variables, to one—a
specific author's word selection—I shall scan the poem that comes
immediately before this one in the collection, *Poisson soluble* no 21, to
determine how many of the linguistic features in question it contains:

*L*es personn*a*ges de *l*a comédie se rass*embl*ent sous un porche,
*l'*ingénue aux accroche-coeur de chè*v*refeuille, *l*a duègne, *l*e
che*v*a*l*ier de cire et *l'en*f*ant* traître. Par-dessus *l*es ruisseaux qui
sont des est*amp*es g*al*antes, *l*es *j*upes s'*env*o*l*ent à moins que
des bras pareils à ceux d'Achi*ll*e ne s'offrent aux be*ll*es à leur
faire tra*v*erser les rue*ll*es. *L*e départ des cor*v*ettes qui *em*portent
*l'*or et *l*es étoffes imprimés est sonné mainte et mainte fois d*ans*
*l*e petit port. *L*e charm*ant* groseillier *en* f*l*eurs qui est un fermier
génér*al* étend *l*en*t*eme*nt l*es bras sur sa couche. Près de *l*ui son
épée est une *l*ibe*ll*u*l*e b*l*eue. Q*uand* i*l* marche, prisonnier des
grâces, *l*es che*v*aux ai*l*és qui piaffent d*ans* son écurie s*embl*ent
prêts à s'*él*a*n*cer d*ans l*es directions *l*es p*l*us fo*ll*es.

Let us now total the number of repeated features:[38]

Poisson soluble 21 ("control" text)	Poisson soluble 22 ("target" text already analyzed)
[ʒ] - 4	[ʒ] - 11
[v] - 6	[v] - 22
[ã] - 16	[ã] - 29

From this simple comparison, we observe that many more of the "pertinent characteristics" of Jean Valjean's name (pertinent to this analysis, at least) recur along the lines of text 22 than in a random text of similar length.[39] These numbers suggest that when a poem seems to be about something *unsaid*, its morphophonemic contours tend to "give away" the secret more readily than would just any other poem. A text that steers the reader towards the subtler level of semiotic functioning through its notable repetition of sub-lexical units, thus rewards him with significant, albeit less suspected, messages. The supplemental messages gleaned from the page reinforce the more general sense he had previously derived from an *inter*textual reading.

Syllabic

The next subdivision in the paragrammatic category, *syllabic,* comprises repetitions of textual unities situated within the boundaries of particular words. Unlike the anagrams just studied, these literary aspects of prose poems repeat only certain parts of the model words, not all of them. Instead of seeking a complete lexical model for this type of copy, the reader isolates a syllable whose poetic function transcends its simple morphemic value. *Le Spleen de Paris* includes at least two texts that contain this kind of feature. The first, "Un plaisant," is set sometime around New Year's:

UN PLAISANT

C'était l'explosion du nouvel an: chaos de boue et de neige, traversé de mille carrosses, étincelant de joujoux et de bonbons, grouillant de cupidités et de désespoirs, délire officiel d'une grande ville fait pour troubler le cerveau du solitaire le plus fort.

Au milieu de ce tohu-bohu et de ce vacarme, un âne trottait vivement, harcelé par un malotru armé d'un fouet.

Comme l'âne allait tourner l'angle d'un trottoir, un beau monsieur ganté, verni, cruellement cravaté et emprisonné dans des habits tout neufs, s'inclina cérémonieusement devant l'humble bête, et lui dit, en ôtant son chapeau: "Je vous la souhaite bonne et heureuse!" puis se retourna vers je ne sais quels camarades avec un air de fatuité, comme pour les prier d'ajouter leur approbation à son contentement.

L'âne ne vit pas ce beau plaisant, et continua de courir avec zèle où l'appelait son devoir.

> Pour moi, je fus pris subitement d'une incommensurable rage
> contre ce magnifique imbécile, qui me parut concentrer en lui
> tout l'esprit de la France.

The special occasion gives the narrator a chance to observe the
official chaos and delirium of a big city during its celebration. In the middle
of the scene, he watches a donkey come trotting by at a fast pace. A
handsome, well-dressed passerby bows down and, with a great deal of
respect, wishes the donkey a happy new year. Suddenly, the narrator flies
into a rage. Seeing the gentleman turn towards friends with an unbearable
air of self-satisfaction, he decides that in this *plaisant* is condensed the
French *esprit*. The man's fatuity, emphasized by his sincerity with an ass,
reminds the narrator of the same contentedness in all his other countrymen.

One inference the reader makes is that the gentleman, *ce magnifique
imbécile,* is really as stupid as the ass he so reverently salutes. Since the
beast does not even see him, the only thing he stands to gain from his action
is some sort of pathetic admiration from his friends. Except for displaying
his social superiority to this humble creature, the man neither accomplishes
nor proves anything at all with his mockery.

On the other hand, the text presents a specific structure to the reader.
If one wanted to plot the prose poem's narrative course, one could describe
it as a progression from New Year's to the ass to the man to the spirit of
France. This progression corresponds to the order in which these subjects
are treated in the various paragraphs. But beyond its mere ordering of events
and characters, the text has graphemic and / or phonemic contours that
establish an equivalence between them. Reviewing the above progression in
its original French form, we find: "nouvel *an*"; "*âne*"; "ce beau plais*ant*";
and "tout l'esprit de la Fr*an*ce." Through a repetition of the sound [ã]
and / or the syllable / an / from the title "Un plais*ant*," the poem puts the
larger unities in which they are found on an equal footing. The noise and
confusion of New Year's Day are re-presented first by a fast moving
donkey, that next becomes formally equated to the man, who finally
embodies the spirit of France:

> Comme l'*â*ne allait tourner l'*an*gle d'un trottoir, un beau
> monsieur g*an*té, verni, cruellem*en*t cravaté et *em*prisonné d*an*s
> des habits tout neufs, s'inclina cérémonieusem*en*t dev*an*t
> l'humble bête, et lui dit, *en* ôt*an*t son chapeau; "je vous la
> souhaite bonne et heureuse!" puis se retourna vers je ne sais
> quels camarades avec un air de fatuité, comme pour les prier
> d'ajouter leur approbation à son cont*en*tem*en*t.

There is a distinct possibility that the poem's only three circumflex accents, those of *âne, humble bête,* and *ôtant son chapeau,* iconographically overdetermine the link between the man and the animal. (Other iconic features will shortly be examined.) Whatever the case, our syllabic repetition certainly constitutes a metonymic chain stretching from the text's title to the last word, France. As such, it underlines the narrator's ambivalence towards his country, an ambivalence that turns into rage when he faces France's more respected citizens, "magnificent imbeciles," like this one.

If Baudelaire's "Le joujou du pauvre" has a moral—in fact, he wrote an earlier piece called "Morale du joujou"—it is simply this: though toys may come in many different shapes and sizes, they are fundamentally the same.[40] Whereas the rich child in the story owns a "joujou splendide, aussi frais que son maître, verni, doré, vêtu d'une robe pourpre, et couvert de plumets et de verroteries," the poor child has a live rat. Nevertheless, as the text makes perfectly clear, both children seem to be more happy with the rat. The rat even lures the wealthy child away from his expensive doll, as would "un objet rare et inconnu." Gazing intently at the box that contains the filthy rodent, "les deux enfants se riaient l'un à l'autre fraternellement, avec des dents d'une *égale* blancheur."

The equality in question here is of course a play on words, seeing that their respective stations in life are hardly equal. Baudelaire recognizes this by italicizing the adjective, which he applies to both children. But though they may not be equal in terms of economic class, in front of their common toy, the two boys smile at each other like brothers. This is where syllabic repetition plays its supplementary role in the text. Having opted for the infantile form *joujou* instead of the "adult" form *jouet,* the author consciously or unconsciously signals a fundamental equality which the entire poem attempts to develop narratively. Since the toy is the great equalizer of otherwise diametrically opposed children, there is an added note of contextual relevance in its being spelled with two identical syllables. While everything else separates them, the *joujou* brings the boys together, equalizes them.

Iconic

The final area of a text in which the reader discovers potentially[41] operative repetitive traits is the one covering letters, accent marks, and punctuation points. Below the punctuation level are found graphic traces that no one (except maybe for carnival "writing analysts") has ever codified or assumed could ever be codified. Previously, I have had occasion to mention this iconic level of poeticity without really developing it. Here, I will demonstrate more specific ways by which such textual signs convey extra meaning in particular prose poems. At issue is not whether these minimal graphemic signs always signify what I shall claim they do, but whether in specific environments, and within a given idiolect, they can act thus.

While it may be impossible to prove that isolated graphemic marks serve as stable representations of precise referents, one should be able (as with any other linguistic unity) to derive some poetic functionality from their repetition *within a context.* Let us take, for instance, Baudelaire's "La Chambre double."[42] Since the room itself never changes, the reader knows that the narrator is the real double. He is doubled up, so to speak, as the before and after of a drug experience. Everything he tells us, therefore, could conceivably echo his psychic duality. Considering the great number of double-letter clusters in the text, e.g., *spirituelle, mirettes, bonne nouvelle,* all of which are italicized, can we assume a stylistic connection with the narrative structure? Perhaps. The problem is that critics are not sure how great the number of such features should be.[43] To take seriously such marginal phenomena would, of course, entail revamping some of their most ingrained reading habits. Before we choose to do that, more examples need to be presented.

Baudelaire's "Chacun sa Chimère" has to do with men walking under a grey sky, on a large, dusty plain. A repetition of the word *sans* in the description of this plain, "sans chemins, sans gazon, sans un chardon, sans une ortie," makes it even more barren than an actual desert. In fact, the reiterated "without" turns this plain into an hyperbole of a desert, and stresses the total sterility of the place through which these wanderers have to pass.[44] Coming from nowhere in particular and going to "où la surface arrondie de la planète se dérobe à la curiosité du regard humain," they are escaping their world physically and metaphysically. Their metaphysical flight is aided by the personal chimera each has on his back. Like the narrator in Baudelaire's prose poem, "Anywhere out of the world," they are unconcerned with their destination.

Yet, even though the chimerae are dream-like presences that help these miserable men escape into dreams, paradoxically, their weight causes them to bend over grotesquely. From the first allusion to these backs to the final line in the poem, the author insists on the bodily curvature that such oppression produces: ". . . je rencontrai plusieurs hommes qui marchaient courbés . . . j'en fus plus lourdement accablés qu'ils ne l'étaient eux-mêmes par leurs écrasantes Chimères." Scanning just one paragraph of the text should suffice to illustrate the iconic value of the grapheme / c / in this regard:

Chose curieuse à noter: aucun de ces voyageurs n'avait l'air irrité contre la bête féroce suspendue à son cou et collée à son dos; on eût dit qu'il la considérait comme faisant partie de lui-même. Tous ces visages fatigués et sérieux ne témoignaient d'aucun désespoir; sous la coupole spleenétique du ciel, les pieds plongés dans la poussière d'un sol aussi désolé que ce ciel, ils cheminaient avec la physionomie résignée de ceux qui sont condamnés à espérer toujours.

This multiplication of an alliterative / c / throughout the poem, which began in the title (originally "Chacun la sienne"), is further accentuated by the capital C in each occurrence of the *Chimère*. Has Baudelaire associated the shape of this letter with the effect of weight on human beings? Apollinaire, who would later play consciously with letters, once put a large / C / in bold-face type to represent that same shape in reference to a lunar crescent.[45]

Modern American poets, too, offer clear-cut examples of / c / being used to express the notion of curvature. E. E. Cummings, in his poem "[space being (don't forget to remember) Curved],"[46] for instance, capitalizes the letter in key words like "Course" and "Creation" to develop his point. Wallace Stevens devotes an entire poem to it entitled, "The Comedian as the letter C."[47] If these other texts do not constitute definitive proof, they at least indicate some symbolic intertextual possibilities inherent in the letter / c /.[48]

Some may dismiss this as an interesting coincidence at best, and serious error at worst. My contention is that the more analysts notice these discrete traits of poeticity, the more crucial becomes the question of their pertinence to the description of a work's style by a particular reader. Ruwet's statement, "le problème de la pertinence des éléments poétiques est loin d'être résolu,"[49] appears increasingly significant in this regard. Indeed, if the preceding paragrammatic features have been pertinent to the general classificatory system of iterative formal traits advanced here, they would seem to be at least qualitatively similar to any more blatant or elaborate, linguistic signals. Hence, the primary criterion of pertinence for a potentially significant feature of poeticity would consist in its functioning on the same epistemological ground, *repetition*, as any other feature. By definition then, each category proposed here would be pertinent to—though certainly not exclusive of—all those readings of literary texts that understand texts as incompletely fathomed depths of multiple, repetitive "speech acts."

In order to isolate more convincing evidence for iconic repetition, let us read another piece from *Le Spleen de Paris,* "Le Thyrse." Written in the form of a description or definition of a thyrsus, the poem dwells on that object's bizarre admixture of straightness and sinuosity. Made up of a stick around which many different flowers are twisted, the thyrsus generates several meditations on the writer's part:

> Ne dirait-on pas que toutes ces corolles délicates, tous ces calices, explosions de senteurs et de couleurs, exécutent un mystique fandango autour du bâton hiératique? . . . Ligne droite et ligne arabesque, intention et expression, roideur de la volonté, sinuosité du verbe, unité du but, variété des moyens, amalgame tout-puissant et indivisible du génie, quel analyste aura le détestable courage de vous diviser et de vous séparer?

Immediately after this lyric *élan,* the text repeats the name of the person to whom its epigraph was addressed, Franz Liszt. Comparing everything evoked by the thyrsus to Liszt's music, the author succeeds in creating a metaphor that could be expressed, *Liszt is a thyrsus.* Now if anyone were wondering why the signifier "Liszt" (above and beyond his historical reality) belongs in this context, he need only consider that name's form. The juxtaposition of / s / and / z / could not be better suited to an iconic description of a thyrsus. Zigzagging in opposite directions, while surrounded by the three straight lines in / l /, / i /, / t /, these two letters represent the very musical and dance arabesques that the rest of the text aims to sketch out.

As a purely formal signal, this repetition allows the reader to conceptualize more vividly a music that he may very well have never heard. Indeed, from a semiotic point of view, it is not necessary for the modern reader to know the referent at all. That Baudelaire and his contemporaries actually thought or spoke about Liszt's music in these metaphorical terms does not alter our perception of the connection his name makes with the thyrsus in the least. As long as we have understood the metaphorical relationship, there is no empirical reason to dispute Liszt's place in it. The shape of his name gives a sufficiently accurate picture both of his music and of a thyrsus.

Rimbaud's "Marine" consists of two sentences that depict vessels cutting through sea and land. In both cases their motion results in the moving aside (or away) of what is left behind:

[. . .]
les courants de la lande.
Et les ornières immenses du reflux,
Filent circulairement vers l'est,
Vers les piliers de la forêt,
Vers les fûts de la jetée [. . .]

The reader who scans this text for repetitive forms suddenly notes one in the / v / of *vers*. In addition, he finds two circumflex accents or inverted v's in the clauses beginning with that word. Seeking out the model for these copies, he is led back to certain intertextual models of a ship's wake.[50] Anyone who has been in a moving boat knows that the triangular shape of the water left sliced behind it, so to speak, resembles an ever-growing / v /.[51] It is thus not far-fetched to think that Rimbaud had this image somewhere in mind, and that it intruded as it were on the surface of his text. That the notion of geometric figures should enter into our reading can also be inferred from the poem's final lines:

Vers les fûts de la jetée,
Dont l'*angle* est heurté par des tourbillons de lumière. (my emphasis)

Ever since Francis Ponge made explicit[52] his iconic use of the circumflex accent in the prose poem "Huître," it is clear that textual signs of this order can add something to a text's literariness. But before critics were even conscious of these poetic aspects, Breton was already unwittingly engaged in experiments with them.[53] The four short examples that follow complete our exploration of formal repetitions, and suggest to what extent the pure materiality of a language (its actual shape as marks on the page) lays the foundation for its "literary" utilization.

I begin with an examination of the giant wasp's voice in *Poisson soluble* no. 3. Of all the expressions Breton might have written to describe the insect's sounds, he chose the syntagm, "chantant à tue-tête." Since the signifier *guêpe* is formed by an extremely rare cluster of graphemic signs, *uê*, it could not easily generate other textual copies. Two notable exceptions that come to mind (both nouns) are *guêtre* and *quête*. The adverbial expression actually present in the poem, however, just happens to repeat the graphemic idiosyncrasy of the word for "wasp." In this sense, the text makes it seem as if singing *à tue-tête* were a unique brand of song reserved for that insect, a loud, quasi-natural "wasp's song."

Poem no. 18 of the same collection introduces another fantastic creature, an ambulatory street lamp (*réverbère*).[54] From the very beginning, a noticeable proliferation of both grave and acute accents in close proximity to one another gives one the idea that *réverbère* generates the greatest part of the textual fabric. The mirroring, or one might say, reverberation of accents repeats the form of the model. Owing to the much higher frequency in French of acute accents over grave, the poem somehow has to compensate. To accomplish this, it presents the reader with a large number of syntagms, often adverbial, that start with the preposition *à*. To cite just a few examples, let us look first at the opening paragraph:

> Le réverbère qui se rapprochait insensiblement du bureau de poste cette nuit-l*à* s'arrêtait *à* chaque instant pour prêter l'oreille. Est-ce *à* dire qu'il avait peur? (emphasis mine)

A second example comes from the middle of the text:

> En effet, dix minutes s'étaient *à peine* écoulées que j'entendis *à nouveau* une chemise, qui devait être verte, glisser lentement du dossier de la chaise de la cabine jusqu'*à terre* où elle vécut quelques temps de la vie d'un chardon, dans le sable, au bord de la mer (emphasis mine).

The most extraordinary effect of these accent marks lies in how they come to be personified by the text. Thanks to an abrupt and inexplicable shift from the post office (which the street lamp approaches) to a bathhouse, two women, later identified as Sonia and Michelle, become the main focus of the narrative. What strikes me as particularly significant here is the way Breton portrays them. Right after learning of the street lamp, we read: "Dans l'*é*tablissement de bains, deux femmes très belles et s*é*v*è*rement maquillées. . . ." The adverb *sévèrement* serves as the initial icon that relates the women back to *réverbère,* as if to say that *réverbère* had some special relationship with *sévèrement.* Subsequent details concerning them confirm the existence of this stylistic feature. The street lamp says: "Sonia et Michelle feront bien de se méfier du rameau de fièvre qui garde les portes de Paris. . . . Mieux vaudrait pour elles éviter la curiosité des lèvres, si elles succombent *à* la tentation des ponts jetés sur les regards. (Je vais les tracer.)"

From a metalinguistic point of view, Breton's last parenthetical comment very nearly exposes the kind of scriptural painting or iconographism which his own text exhibits. If the narrative voice traces anything, it is the signifier "bridges." This signifier has apparently been derived from a rearrangement of the scrambled, albeit absent expressions *jeter des ponts sur,* and *jeter des regards sur* into the phrase *jeter des regards sur des ponts.*

This act of glancing at the icons of bridges (as perhaps in "draw bridges" or *pont-levis*) describes exactly what the reader does when noting the text's accents. He reads them, or, more precisely, sees them as he would the raising and lowering (*ponts jetés*) of a bridge from opposite sides. Thus the narrative concludes on what amounts to a putting-into-perspective of the poem's formal gymnastics. Referring back first to the women, and next to the street lamp metonyms, i.e., mirrors, it repeats the pattern *accents aigus - accents graves*:

> Ces deux femmes m'ont appartenu tout un jour que je finissais ténébreusement d'être jeune. Et me voici, proph*è*t*e à* la tempe plus pure que les miroirs, enchaîné par les lueurs de mon histoire, couvert d'amours glaçantes, en proie aux fantasmagories de la baguette brisée et demandant que par pitié, d'un seul brillant final, on me ramène *à* la vie. (emphasis mine)

Also owing to its accent pattern, the adverb *ténébreusement*, infrequently used in French (except in mysterious tales such as we enter into at the very beginning of this poem), represents here a highly appropriate signifier in this stylistic environment. Followed closely by the group "prophète *à*," with its two *accents graves*, it acts as a kind of accent-mirror producing a specular image of stereo-isometric accents.

Poisson soluble no. 10 reveals an artist's tendency to happen upon even punctuation marks as worthy models to copy. A propos of the unusual wall of a crate, the narrator remarks: ". . . l'on m'a affirmé qu'un berger, où l'on se serait attendu à lire Fragile, a lu Paul et Virginie. Oui Paul et Virginie, *point* et *virgule*." (emphasis mine). Not only do the words for the period and comma repeat the initial letters of the names, Paul and Virginie, they also repeat the punctuation marks that surround them. It is even likely that there is additional formal cause for this stylistic aspect, a cause or model we can find in the colon that introduces the above quotation, "Une remarque curieuse: [. . .]." The term for colon in French is, of course, *deux points*.

My final example of iconic repetition (final because I cannot detect any smaller graphemic traces on the page) is one formed by the hyphens in Breton's prose poem no. 28.[55] Commencing with Saint-Cloud, and continuing with *hommes-cages, infra-rouge, chambre-Paris,* the text deals with the vagaries of a high-speed car trip. The moral of the trip, according to the work itself, is that *"dans le temps il n'y a plus de droite ni de gauche,"* a phrase italicized in the poem. Given the nature of hyphens, the moral would appear to undermine the text's insistence on them. After all, one cannot say Cloud-Saint instead of Saint-Cloud and still "make sense." Yet, can we really say that *cages-hommes* is any less meaningful than *hommes-cages*? I think not. The intratextual repetition of hyphens thereby intensifies a point that the poem is trying to make somewhere else, just as all the other features we have studied up until now.

Thus, the smaller the textual unity under investigation, the more problematic its existence. Lacking a "paragrammatic" dictionary, we are forced to grope for these supplementary poetic aspects in relative darkness. I say "relative" because, compared to more attested semantic components of an utterance, they enjoy less critical acceptance. In the light of our findings, however, they seem to depend no more or less on the iterative phenomenon than do the former. To the extent that they are signs belonging primarily to the message, and not to the code (*langue*), they deserve much fuller treatment than that accorded to isolated, un-repeated features. For as Linda Waugh indicates:

> it is simply *not* the case that all linguistic signs belong to the code. *Many* belong only to the message. Thus, the equation between code [*langue*] and sign [of a *parole*, or what we have been calling an *idiolect*], which is assumed in some linguistic and literary studies, is not valid. . . . A distinction between message [*parole*] and the usage to which a given message may be put has to be made.[56]

This last clause, "the usage to which a given message may be put," reminds us of our earlier questions vis-à-vis the pertinence of sub-lexical features in the description of a text's poeticity. It reminds us that our status as literary critics depends in part on their consideration.

NOTES

[1]*CLG*, p. 34.

[2]The most important of whom is Derrida, who does not interpret so much as he does write the trace of a trace. Interpretation for Derrida implies acceptance of an absolute meaning, which we know he rejects. As a result, his type of interpretation, deconstruction, consists of copying what can be understood only as other copies.

[3]Such uncertainty can make all the difference between reading a work as poetic or as non-poetic. Indeed, one could read the typographical schemes of whole texts in the same way we read discursive intertextuality in chapter two. By simply glancing at the overall shape a text takes on a single piece of paper, a reader can often surmise (before actually reading it through completely) that he is in the presence of a prose poem, blank verse, free verse, etc. For more thorough treatment of this issue, see Daniel Delas and Jacques Filliolet, *Linguistique et Poétique* (Paris: Larousse, 1973), p. 168.

[4]A similar problem of identification arises in another of Baudelaire's prose poems, "Laquelle est la vraie?"

[5]See the section "L'un dans l'autre" in André Breton's *Perspective Cavalière* (Paris: Gallimard, 1970) for several examples of this game. In essence, the game consists of a secret word like "sword" which an individual has to guess based on clues he gets from an image of this word that a group comes up with spontaneously. This particular word led some of Breton's friends to talk about a necktie. The notion of a fixed tenor / vehicle structure in metaphor is thus subverted since the two poles in this surrealist game are more or less arbitrarily selected.

[6]Lautréamont, whose work Breton was among the first to admire, often availed himself of such geometric imagery. See, for example, the opening stanzas of *Les Chants de Maldoror* or pp. 106-10 for similar geometric figures.

[7]Since Breton dubs this line "la perpendiculaire de Dieu" it recalls Baudelaire's characterization of a clock in the poem, "L'Horloge": "Horloge! *dieu* sinistre, effrayant, impassible. . ." (emphasis mine). With each passing second, the sinister god Time divides into tiny segments what would otherwise be a continuous, atemporal state.

[8]We are not far from the kind of pictorial style found in *Calligrammes*, except that Apollinaire was more conscious and deliberate in his exploitation of such imagery than his "disciple" Breton.

[9]Bernard, *Le Poème en prose*, p. 203.

[10]See appendix for entire text, pp. 141-142.

[11]Riffaterre arrives at the same conclusion, but bases it entirely on the second section. While I do not deny the text's capacity to "give itself away" sooner, I wonder if Riffaterre's previous knowledge of the rest of the poem did not aid him in his particular analysis. As I contend in section three of my final chapter, the critic is precisely he who *has* reread. See *Semiotics of Poetry*, pp. 120-22.

[12]Although I have not been able personally to make the connections, it is to be supposed that the repeated lines "Un souffle disperse les limites du foyer..." ("Nocturne Vulgaire"), "Le pavillon en viande saignante..." ("Barbare"), and many others in the Rimbaldian corpus have analogous formal roles to play in their respective texts. As Nicolas Ruwet puts it: "...n'arrive-t-il pas que les parallélismes, au lieu seulement de se superposer aux principes "ordinaires" [sémantico-pragmatiques], s'y substituent? [On] est amené à chercher un lien sémantique entre les éléments que, précisément rien ne relie sémantiquement, mais qui sont mis en parallélisme syntaxique. . . ." Quoted from Nicolas Ruwet, "Parallélismes et déviations en poésie," in *Langue, Discours, Société* (Paris: Seuil, 1975), pp. 317-19.

[13]Hoping to avoid any misconception of my terminology, I use this term in its strict etymological sense of "running alongside the line."

[14]Anthony Johnson, "Anagrammatism in Poetry: Theoretical Preliminaries," *PTL*, 2 (1977), 101.

[15]The expression is Riffaterre's. See his analysis of the repeated word *passer* in Queneau's poem "Héraldique" in *Semiotics of Poetry*, p. 108.

[16]Julia Kristéva, "La Productivité dite texte," *Communications*, 11 (1968), 74.

[17]Quoted in Jean Cohen, "Poésie et redondance," *Poétique*, 28 (1976), 416. Cohen disagrees with Kristéva because he believes that lexical repetition increases a so-called "effet affectif," not "le sens noétique," of a work. For my part, I find terms like the former far too subjective to be of any real value in a formal theory of literariness. There is simply no way to quantify feelings.

[18]Michel Foucault notes, "La répétition n'est cherchée et trouvée qu'à partir de cette infime différence qui induit paradoxalement l'identité . . ." in his *Raymond Roussel* (Paris: Gallimard, 1963), p. 35.

[19]Cf. Barbara Johnson, "Quelques conséquences des différences anatomiques des textes," p. 463: "Le mot clé du poème en vers, "confondues" cède la place, dans le poème en prose, au mot "combinées": le modèle totalisant des vers devient simplement, métonymiquement, *additif*."

[20]This term, used by Barbara Johnson, was derived from her reading of Suzanne Bernard's analysis of the prose poem and verse poem versions of Baudelaire's "Invitation au voyage." See Johnson's *The Critical Difference*, p. 24.

[21]Johnson, *The Critical Difference*, p. 43

[22]See Riffaterre's key study of this kind of metaphor in *La Production du texte*, pp. 217-34.

[23]That such a stylistic anomaly occurs at all might be explained as the textual trace of an unconscious preoccupation on Breton's part with this rhetorical trope. *Apostrophe* means "to turn away from."

[24]Adjectives like Baudelairean, Rimbaldian, etc., attribute more control to the poet over his language than he perhaps has. For this reason, it would be safer to talk simply about the imagery or vocabulary in their works rather than in their psyches.

[25]Riffaterre, *Semiotics of Poetry*, pp. 117-19.

[26]Being parts of the descriptive system attached to the act of juggling, fingers (and therefore nails) are *semantically* linked to it as well. I thank Professor LeRoy C. Breunig of Barnard College for pointing this out to me. Nevertheless, this additional, overdetermining aspect appears secondary in view of the comparison's formal logic.

[27]Michael Riffaterre, *Essais de stylistique structurale*, p. 277.

[28]The ending -*ika* recalls several Dutch, Germanic, and Scandinavian names.

[29]Sylvère Lotringer explains: "L' 'anagramme' n'est pas à définir comme une dislocation réglée en mal de complétude, mais comme une multiplicité infixable, indécidabilité radicale qui défait tous les codes." In "Le 'complexe' de Saussure," *Semiotext(e)*, 2, No. 1 (1975), 112.

[30]To say that it can be does not mean that it *will* be. However, the same holds true for many other features that do not actually appear in the visible form of a text's graphemes. Any analysis leading to an unsaid semantic matrix, for example, though infinitely more verifiable (hence credible), is contingent on the linguistic and literary competence of the critic who performs it. As such, it presupposes a certain give and take between reader and text. But how does one quantify what one must give or bring to a work in order to get back a particular interpretation? When can one be sure that his competence is sufficiently developed to notice *every* significant aspect?

[31]Robert Sabatier, *La Poésie du Moyen Age* (Paris: Editions Albin Michel, 1975), p. 21.

[32]Cohn makes the very same observation. But, for reasons unclear to me, he is satisfied with its mere mention, and goes no further. See *The Poetry of Rimbaud,* pp. 282-83.

[33]*Ibid*. Cohn notes this, too.

[34]Though the examples of anagrams in Rimbaud may seem less probable than this one, the contextual clues (e.g., *Vies, saint*, etc.) were not qualitatively different from these here. The question, once again, is how much effort is too much to exert in order to recover what is not said by a text?

[35]We can justify the inversion on the basis of the commutative law of logic as well as the inverted interrogative form, *est-ce*.

[36]Chrétien de Troyes, *Le Chevalier de la Charrette*, trans. Jean Frappier (Paris: Champion, 1971), pp. 128-130.

[37]Riffaterre, *La Production du texte*, pp. 244–49.

[38]I disregard the letter / 1 / in my analysis because of its normally high frequency in French articles. Contrary to the repeated letters / v / and / j /, / 1 / is much less likely to provoke any reaction in the unsuspecting reader.

[39]It will have been remarked that I skipped several lines in my transcription of the text 22 in which I determined this paragrammatic feature to be operative. One might argue that I thereby increased the length of the passage, and added another variable to the discussion. Since my comparison depends more, however, on a similar number of random words than on their particular combination, the exact order of these words need not figure among the experimental parameters.

[40]See Appendix for the entire poem, p. 143.

[41]My reticence is occasioned by the speculative nature of my readings. There are as yet no books, no rules, no conventions governing such minuscule signs. However, this does not mean that they do not *in fact* function on some level of the writer's, *and* any given reader's mind.

[42]See Appendix for entire poem, pp. 144-145.

[43]Susan Suleiman encounters this same problem in her "Redundancy and the Readable Text," *Poetics Today*, 1, III (Spring 1980), 119-142. On page 140 she states that "excessive redundancy" (her term) is a "relative, and therefore variable, concept." My statistical comparison of the phonemes and graphemes in the two prose poems in *Poisson soluble* serves as a preliminary response to this question of how one determines how many repetitions are "enough" for them to be semiotically significant.

[44]Cf. Baudelaire's verse poem "Bohémiens en Voyage" for an analogous description of wanderers.

[45]In his text "Voyage" in Guillaume Apollinaire, *Calligrammes* (Paris: Gallimard, 1925), p. 55.

[46]Quoted from *The Norton Anthology of Modern Poetry*, ed. Richard Ellman and Robert O'Clair (New York and London: W. W. Norton and Company, 1973), p. 535.

[47]Wallace Stevens, *The Collected Poems of Wallace Stevens* (New York: Knopf, 1955), pp. 27-46.

[48]Since this kind of phenomenon is born of what Kristéva calls *la productivité* (as opposed to *la production*), it belongs outside of the realm of the likely. As she says, "la vérité de la productivité n'est pas prouvable ni vérifiable, ce qui voudrait dire que la productivité textuelle relève d'un domaine autre que le vraisemblable . . . elle consiste dans *l'accomplissement* du geste productif, c'est-à-dire du trajet scriptural se faisant et se détruisant lui-même . . .", in "La productivité dite texte," p. 81.

[49]*Langage, Musique, Poésie*, p. 216.

⁵⁰As we find in Baudelaire's poem, "Don Juan aux Enfers." There Don Juan is said to be navigating across a black ocean, while observing the clearly defined wake (*sillage*) of his boat. By virtue of its being reproduced in a literary text, this familiar v-shape acts as a typical literary representation of what happens to water behind a boat.

⁵¹Mallarmé provides us with this sample of the iconic "cutting" power of the letter / v /:

> Le vierge, le vivace et le bel aujourd'hui
> Va-t-il nous déchirer d'un coup d'aile ivre,
> Ce lac dur oublié que hante sous le givre
> Le transparent glacier des vols qui n'ont pas fui!

In Stéphane Mallarmé, *Poésies* (Paris: Gallimard, 1945), p. 123.

⁵²See *Entretiens de Francis Ponge avec Philippe Sollers* (Paris: Gallimard-Seuil, 1970), pp. 111-12. Ponge explains that his use of words like *blanchâtre, opiniâtre,* and *verdâtre* was determined to a large extent by a combination of the accent and the letters / tre / in the title.

⁵³Before him I find José-Maria de Hérédia. In his poem, "Antoine et Cléopâtre" the only *accents circonflexes* to appear are those in the title, and in an ambiguous verse that reads: "Tournant sa tête pâle entre ses cheveux bruns." Although the reader cannot be sure, grammatically speaking, whose head this is, the repeated accents suggest that it is Cleopatra's. As it happens, the text verifies this in the very next two verses. Quoted from José-Maria de Hérédia, *Les Trophées* (Cambridge: Cambridge University Press, 1946), p. 32. I do a more complete analysis of this poem in chapter four, pp. 113-118.

⁵⁴See Appendix for the complete three-page poem, pp. 146-147.

⁵⁵See Appendix for complete text, p. 148-149.

⁵⁶See Linda Waugh, "The Poetic Function in the Theory of Roman Jakobson," *Poetics Today,* 2, No. 1a (1980), 61-2.

Chapter IV

USAGE OF THE TYPOLOGY AND REVISED DEFINITIONS

The linguistic categories elaborated in this study provide a general, if inexhaustive, scheme by which a great many stylistic features of prose poems arise from (intertextually) and give rise to (intratextually) other stylistic features. Hierarchical in nature, this scheme takes the shape of a kind of generative tree of poeticity that looks like this:

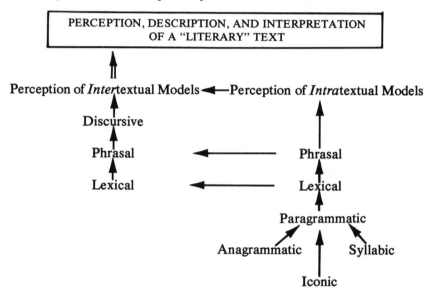

As the arrows suggest, subtle stylistic aspects of a literary work tend to support more textually-extensive aspects which a reader usually finds easier to identify on the page. The reason these more extensive features—generated by words, phrases, and entire discourses—are easier to identify is that they already have the status of verifiable, understandable communicational units. To say that such units can be verified and understood must not be construed, however, as meaning they will accept only one correct interpretation. Linguists have repeatedly shown that even the simplest of utterances provokes a wide range of interpretative reactions in the listener/reader.

So when I contend, for instance, that the narrator in "Le Mauvais Vitrier" takes literally the phrases *casser les verres,* or *casser les vitres*, and creates his entire narrative out of a fusion of this expression's denotative and connotative planes, my statement does not in any way invalidate

Barbara Johnson's reading the same narrative as a pun on the word pair *vers-verres*. Nor does it refute her concomitant invocation of the prose poem / verse poem distinction. Yet, even though our two interpretations are based on equally close readings, and derive their validity from the same grapho-phonemic stimuli, they are not equivalent. For by the same means we arrive at different ends.

As it happens, our two readings have something more important in common than the simple fact that they focus in on the same details. They both proceed from a critical appraisal of a phrasal intertextual repetition, a model-copy unit. While her model, "casser les *vers*," was different from mine, her textual copy was the same, "casser les *verres*." If the particular entries we chose within this conceptual paradigm (phrasal) were dissimilar, we still comprehended them, therefore, in terms of the same function or linguistic process. The motives for our dissimilar selections are, of course, still open to investigation.

Specifically then, what our scheme illustrates is that the ultimate perception, description, and interpretation of a given piece of writing as a "literary" text occur through a notation of the many levels on which formal iteration of *other* literature takes place. It forms the beginning stage of a more comprehensive description of the linguistic frames any symbolic articulation needs in order to transmit messages of varying significance to different readers. If Julia Kristéva's semiotic realm is that Platonic *chora* of undifferentiated, pre-symbolic impulses at work in a writer's mind and body, then our typology is a more contemporary sketch than hers of its symbolic counterpart, its transposition[1] or putting-into-language.

Since one can never really know what these impulses are anyway, one might at least try to describe their functioning in language. That is, while we can never be sure whether Baudelaire in "Le Mauvais Vitrier" was, for some psycho-sexual reason, exhibiting a sense of black humour; or whether, instead, he was anxious to illustrate graphically the prose poem / verse poem dichotomy for his fellow poets, we can be minimally assured that he demonstrated *it* through phrasal gymnastics. The "what" of what he was *attempting* to express thus gives way, in our scheme, to the way in which it was expressed.

Now if the various levels of formal iteration allow us to describe a text as literary, it is because these levels are the observable writing dimensions in which, sooner or later, more conventional stylistic features of other literature appear. The temporal parameter introduced by this adverbial qualifier recalls our earlier distinction between past and future repetitions, as well as the idea that an intratextual feature is the sign of an eventual intertextual one. A text will be considered literary, in other words, on the basis of the multiple ways it copies, intertextually, facets of other already-accepted literature. As a consequence, we might suppose that any examination of works from genres historically more esteemed than prose poems would yield similar results, similar model-copy pairs at work. Such an examination should uncover all of the different levels of iteration explored so far. We should therefore be able to adduce certain stylistic features perhaps previously suspected, but not fully elaborated in the genre we choose to examine.

To this end, we might profitably direct our attention to the sonnet. This fixed form, or, if one prefers, discursive practice, lies at the other end of the genre gamut represented earlier by the prose poem. Having a rigid structure, complete with strict versification and, often, thematic constraints, the sonnet lends itself easily to a detailed study of sub-discursive levels of formal iteration. Since the discursive level of the sonnet has already been investigated and described by countless critics, it would be of some use to a general theory of the literary phenomenon to see whether the other categories proposed here continue to operate in so strict a form. If they do, we will be in a good position to accept the fact that in any type or genre of literature there are at least as many levels of formal iteration producing meaning for different readers as presented so far. These levels would, in their turn, provide adequate exploratory territory for further research into the specifics of each category.

* * *

To illustrate how our scheme can be applied to a literary text outside of the prose poem corpus, I should like to study at greater length a sonnet mentioned in an earlier analysis, José-Maria de Hérédia's "Antoine et Cléopâtre." Here is the complete text:

ANTOINE ET CLÉOPÂTRE

Tous deux ils regardaient, de la haute terrasse,
L'Egypte s'endormir sous un ciel étouffant
Et le Fleuve, à travers le Delta noir qu'il fend,
Vers Bubaste ou Saïs rouler son onde grasse.

Et le Romain sentait sous la lourde cuirasse,
Soldat captif berçant le sommeil d'un enfant,
Ployer et défaillir sur son coeur triomphant
Le corps voluptueux que son étreinte embrasse.

Tournant sa tête pâle entre ses cheveux bruns
Vers celui qu'enivraient d'invincibles parfums,
Elle tendit sa bouche et ses prunelles claires;

Et sur elle courbé, l'ardent Imperator
Vit dans ses larges yeux étoilés de points d'or
Toute une mer immense où fuyaient des galères.

On the intertextual level, there are three primary categories of iterative traits that we can begin to examine, just as with the prose poems. The first, discursive, includes all those stylistic features about the present text that copy traits from the genre or fixed form named "sonnet." With reference to various set requirements of a conventional sonnet, the reader will analyze and describe Hérédia's poem in terms of its success or failure to emulate established patterns. The degree of success or failure to copy these patterns will also help to classify the poem as belonging to particular aesthetic movements or schools. Here we have a case of a perfectly standard parnassian sonnet. Its formal structure faithfully reproduces this specific pattern in terms of: 1) the rhyme scheme, 2) number of syllables, 3) alternation of masculine and feminine rhymes, and 4) "noble" subject-matter. Minimally then, the reader interprets the discursive intertextual dimension of this text on the basis of a previously described linguistic, and especially literary form known as "sonnet."

Below or inside this dimension is located the phrasal level of intertextuality. Here the phrase "le Romain sentait sous la lourde cuirasse," for instance, is read in the context of clichés, and stereotypical descriptions of Anthony's shields and / or other quasi-epic heroes' clothing. One can go all the way back to Homer's celebrated description of Achilles's shield in *The Iliad*,[2] or to Virgil's copy in his description of Aeneas's shield in *The Aeneid* for some early examples of this intertextual motif. The question any literary theorist would eventually have to deal with would thus not be so much what Hérédia *means* in using this specific variant of the said description of epic personages' shields, as it would be what the individual reader is able to derive from the (phrasal) form this "meaning" takes. Divergent interpretations of the line, in other words, would seem to grow out of divergent reckonings—at different moments of the reading act—with the textual signifiers located within the same phrasal intertextual category.

The third linguistic paradigm of such formal repetition across textual boundaries lies on the lexical plane. In the reading instant when this phenomenon is noted, a word like *invincibles* in her *invincibles parfums* repeats both a socially recognized metaphoric sense of the word, as with "her irresistible perfumes," *and* the literal sense of in-*vincible*. Seeing the distinct Roman context of Hérédia's poem, one could get few more appropriate lexical entries in this adjectival slot for a charm that seduced two of the most eminent Romans associated with conquests of various sorts, Anthony and Julius Caesar ("veni, vidi, *vici*"). Whether I have interpreted this form correctly, of course, has little to do with the fact that my analysis could not have begun without appraisal of a specific linguistic instance known as a word. Moreover, I do not doubt that ideology determines much of the reader's and writer's activity centered on this and other linguistic frames proposed herein. I shall have more to say about this matter in the third part of this chapter.

When a part of the present text under scrutiny does not immediately recall an aspect of past texts, then we assume that the model one perceives in a "copy" must be located within the work's own graphemic confines. The syntactical elements of the end of verse 5, *sous la lourde cuirasse,* for example, are copied by the end of verse 7, *sur son coeur triomphant.* In both instances, the phrasal components are similar, though not in the same order (prep.-adj.-substantive). Our prior notation of the discursive inter-textual debt this poem has with the sonnet forces us thereby to underline the structural relationship between the prepositions "under" and "over," since they are situated in equivalent positions in the poem.

In this erotic context, where Anthony feels the bending and swooning of this seductress's body, this phrasal intratextual phenomenon commences the *intra*textual domain of the reader's perception of Hérédia's work. Because this "internal" dimension of the text's specificity would not mean much at all were it not connected, sooner or later, to some other text or textual aspect from a different origin, formal intratextuality depends ultimately on intertextuality for its signifying functions. With respect to the reader's act more than to the writer's, this is just another way of saying that literary criticism consists of re-reading; or, more precisely, re-*writing*. For the critic takes the language of a poem, novel, essay and transforms it—through his or her perception of certain psychological, historical, and ideological models—into his or her own meta-language, which replaces and even dis-places the original text. In any case, this under / over distinction in Hérédia's poem would seem to re-invoke the up / down directions usually associated with the sexual act, making it a significant and supplementary stylistic aspect of the poem.

Below this phrasal level of intratextuality is situated the *lexical* level, on which we can isolate aspects like the rhymed pairs *terrasse / grasse, cuirasse / embrasse, bruns / parfums,* etc. The grapho-phonemic similarity of the terms, as well as their rhymed positions, will lead many readers to seek out semantic relationships between them. This interpretative strategy is something not altogether overlooked in the *writing* of sonnets since Petrarch. And yet there are even more textually-specific lexical items in Hérédia's poem that copy other such items. Let us take the adjective "heavy" (*lourde*), for instance, used in reference to Anthony's shield. This adjective can be said to repeat metonymically the adjective "fat" (*grasse*) used earlier to describe the River's waves. Once the internal connection is made, a hermeneutic leap "outwards" occurs to the intertextual realm; that is, provided the perception and interpretation of the work have not ceased. The reader might in that instant wonder whether this lexical repetition could signify an equivalence between the River and Anthony. Indeed, to further the analysis, one could assert that the "black Delta" against which the River thrusts itself replaces, metaphorically, Cleopatra. Needless to say, there is much eroticism already implied before we even reach the previously mentioned scene, where the queen's bodily movements against Anthony's shield are described.

Delving deeper into the text's semiotic "boiling depths," the reader arrives at the final sub-lexical level of formal iteration, the paragrammatic. By this designation I have been referring to three different types of phenomena, all transpiring in the reading-spaces produced by a word's component parts. The first, having a central affiliation with the Saussurean notion, was dubbed anagrammatic. With this kind of intratextual repetition, certain key phonemes and graphemes reiterate an explicit word, e.g., Anthony and Cleopatra, or presupposition of present words, like "love" or "sex," that constitutes a model which the given set of features copies. The set in question could consist of a few words or of several verses considered together. From the strictly linguistic and literary points of view, the validity of such approaches can rarely be refuted.

However, they cannot be proven easily either. What they both depend on is a deduced or restituted model that is nowhere present, and always already inscribed on a particular reader's psyche; and, perhaps, on his or her psyche *alone*. It should nonetheless be supposed that statistical analysis[3] of grapho-phonemic frequencies could yield significant results for a reader-oriented study about the likelihood that a particular anagram in a literary work appear "pertinent" to, or even be noticed by, a portion of the reading audience.

Akin to the latter paragrammatic type of intratextual feature is a second category, syllabic. To recall its definition, this kind of iterative phenomenon unfolds when the reader notes a copying of only a segment of a specific word, and then attempts to explain it in reference to something else. Let us consider the following lines from Hérédia's sonnet:

Et le Fleuve, à tra*vers* le Delta noir qu'il fend,
Vers Bubaste ou Saïs rouler son onde grasse. (my emphasis)

The mere repetition of the syllable / vers / draws attention to itself, and invites the reader of this poem—as did the more visible iterative traits—to perceive the possible significance this syllabic textual insistence has for the poem's overall semantic and semiotic functioning. In view of our earlier intertextual reading of the sonnet, we are justified in interpreting this perceived model / copy pair as a supplementary index of the expressed narrative situation that has Anthony moving *towards* (*vers*) Cleopatra in the next quatrain.

The third and often least obtrusive of the paragrammatic features is the iconic. On this level of the literary text, which is barely defined, though likely perceived by several readers, the repeated presence of a particular letter, diacritical mark, or even punctuation point may eventually induce a critic to seek out a model that would explain its pertinence to the present work. The reason it acts this way is that a given reader may, on the same epistemological grounds (repetition) as with the other linguistic paradigms already examined, posit a significant relationship between the shape of the individual graphic character, and some other shape that belongs to a different text, a different code.

To illustrate the iconic potential of literature's signifiers, I should like to analyze the possible semiotic function of the repeated circumflex accents in line nine of Hérédia's poem: "Tournant sa tête pâle entre ses cheveux bruns. . . ." The reader of iterative linguistic forms will immediately become aware that this intratextual feature may be pointing to something significant beyond itself. The mere usage of two such accent marks side by side already represents a relatively low-frequency textual phenomenon in the French language. And indeed, the only other occurrence of this accent in the entire poem is in the name *Cléopâtre* of the title.

Yet what makes this iconic feature particularly important in the present context is the ambiguity of its reference. Given the syntax, one cannot ascertain just whose head is turning until the next line, "Vers *celui* qu'enivraient . . .". From what the words in line nine themselves denote, one does not know whether it is Cleopatra's head or Anthony's that turns. But when one finally learns that Hérédia was speaking all along about Cleopatra's head, an extraordinary connection takes place in the reader's mind. The repeated and juxtaposed circumflex accents of the group *tête pâle* reinvoke the almost phantom-like presence, or narrative silhouette, if one prefers, of the queen Cleopatra. It accomplishes this by referring back to the unusual graphemic nature of her French name.

At the same time, it lures us into seeing her imagined head, and especially its metonymically associated *head-dress,* in the very form of the repeated accent mark. No other diacritical mark could function so effectively in supplementing the semiotic force of this head portrait. Even in Modern French, one refers to a circumflex accent as a "hat," *chapeau.*

In these ways then, our preliminary typology can be used to describe and analyze the poeticity of types of literature other than the prose poem. To the extent that this typology is inexhaustive, one might suspect the existence of several sub-divisions within the stylistic dimensions elaborated so far. I should therefore further explain now the theoretical need for additional stylistic domains which are equally grounded in the linguistic fabric of the poetic text.

Every type of discourse, fixed form, and genre constitutes a point of departure for a critical iterative typology that is more attuned, as it were, to the particulars of that discourse. Given the conventional aspects of a classical play, a meditation, an elegy, and the like, the sub-discursive levels of typologies specific to them should be peculiar to the actual type of text studied. As a consequence, any expansion of our classificatory system involves mainly quantitative rather than qualitative considerations. In the case of a seventeenth-century play, for example, an enjambment of one verse onto another could be construed as being a faulty, hence significant, phrasal copy of a "proper" twelve-foot line. Any critical comments concerning the enjambment would thus result directly from the requisite notation of a phrasal intertextual phenomenon peculiar to the specific discursive practice known as "classical play." That is, the phrasal level of the typology used in that particular study would have parameters, e.g., twelve syllables, not necessarily pertinent to an interpretation of a similar phrasal structure found in, say, a novel.

Since one is always prepared for a different set of phrasal parameters, depending on the genre of the literary text in question, every textual sequence, from two-word syntagms to elaborate independent / dependent clause structures, can thus function as a phrasal model that is copied by a certain poetic feature in a work. With respect to Rimbaud's "Dévotion," for instance, the genre alerts the reader to the fact that somewhere in the poem he should expect to find a copy of the two word pattern "to X." Similarly, when a reader of Proust associates the latter's highly complex syntactic structures with those of Péguy,[4] there too we are in the presence of phrasal intertextuality, albeit on a much larger scale. An expanded iterative typology would therefore have to account both intertextually and intratextually for all the possible poetic functions of various-sized phrasal units between these two extremes.

On the lexical side, one still needs to determine whether there are other ways in which a word repeats another word, either from the inside or outside of a specific work. In our study, we have seen how intertextual stylistic features sometimes develop out of certain repeated words or out of their presuppositions, metonyms, and even antonyms. But there is no reason to assume that the number of letters in a word, or the particular arrangement of its letters, or even the presence of certain letters and accent marks in the word does not also serve as those pertinent characteristics that make other kinds of copies possible. In the intratextual lexical analyses of chapter three, these were precisely the criteria used in formulating that category. Yet, at the present stage of my research, I do not know whether the above stylistic phenomena actually exhaust the iterative possibilities intrinsic to words. I must, as a result, suspend my inquiry into the matter here, stating merely that much work remains to be done on the different numbers and combinations of the above lexical aspects at work in the reading and writing of single words in literary texts.

As for the sub-lexical levels of the typology, Anthony Johnson has gone the farthest so far, I believe, in describing what he calls "reciprocal" or "secondary anagrammatism."[5] His findings suggest that within my general paragrammatic category one could locate several finer levels on which such formal play occurs. These levels would be defined in terms of their predictability by, and visibility to, the reader. Investigating these supplementary dimensions of signification necessitates a final expansion of our repetition hierarchy. In this last instance, I am talking about an expansion of the syllabic, anagrammatic, and iconic layers of texts. I can think of fewer more promising areas of the literary phenomenon left to explore in depth, and of fewer less fully appreciated at the present time.

* * *

One may have noted that the types of formal iteration this essay attempts to classify often resemble more conventional rhetorical and critical concepts. In this regard, it might be asked how the terms *discursive, phrasal,* or *lexical intertextual repetition* make life any easier for students and critics accustomed to words like "genre," "parody," "allusion," and "irony." To this I would answer that the proposed typology has the distinct advantage of reducing the vast majority of literature's stylistic features to their functional common denominator, repetition. Through a reduction to linguistic models I have tried to suggest that the comprehension and appreciation of literary style derive from different interpretive reckonings with different-sized segments of a discourse.

Once again, I am not saying that we all can or should interpret a work in the same way. I am merely pointing out that we can, and often do, delimit the purely linguistic context of a work in more or less the same fashion before going on to do our respective "readings." This delimitation involves a hermeneutic preoccupation with at least as many linguistic levels of a text as have been illustrated here. Thus, unlike an ever-growing catalogue or rhetoric of the *different* stylistic traits found in a poetic text, our classification explains these same differences in terms of theoretically infinite, but pragmatically finite, functional relationships between identities. The identities to which I refer are quantitatively, not qualitatively, different linguistic models and copies. The very notion of a *relationship,* after all, expresses a conceptual affinity with formal iteration. Etymologically, it means the "act of carrying something back again." Insofar as these relationships are always subtended by some kind of paradigmatic repetition, it would therefore appear less problematic for the theorist to describe and define them by pinpointing the function they all perform (repetition), rather than by groping for the multifarious ways in which they all differ.

I have now reached the point in my discussion where I need to justify in some measure my choice of certain textual repetitions (linguistic) over others. From the very beginning of chapter one, I have insisted that, more than any other factor, a critic's ideological stance determines which of a host of iterative signals in a text will be considered worthy of his or her consideration. Why then all of this emphasis here on the linguistic aspects of a work? Put simply, there is no other dimension of literary or, for that matter, "non-literary" texts upon which students of literature can more effectively come to agree. That is to say, nothing else about a text seems to impose itself on the consciousness of readers with more authority, objectivity, or indeed, *reality*, than the actual words of which it is composed. My personal ideological stance, in other words, is based on the belief that a common ground exists in the reading and, especially, interpretation of literature. It emphasizes not so much the desirability as it does the inevitability of a certain authority, objectivity, and validity in criticism. While the latter statement may sound unfounded, it amounts to no more or less than an affirmation of the capacity of a text's language to signify something, somehow, to someone.

Does this notion of a common ground undermine my often sympathetic attitude towards deconstructionist theory? Not at all. To say that readers of texts have something in common with each other is not the same as saying that they can or should arrive at identical interpretations. This is because, in the final analysis, readers hold in common much of the medium that a particular text merely traverses; to wit, the language (French, English, etc.)

in which it is written. Any given text, therefore, speaks to, but does not necessarily *communicate* equivalently with, all its readers.

So while neither the reader nor the text is a completely fixed pole, they do share something linguistic. Any reader who describes, analyzes, and interprets a poetic trait, in other words, does so on the primary basis of a text's language. As a result, it can be reasonably asserted that he or she shares a series of commonly identified linguistic frames with other readers. Sooner or later in the act of criticism, a specific individual's ideology will permeate and color these same frames, but not without permitting the theorist to delineate the linguistic contours of the poetic traits they "contain," as it were. Thus, the main goal in choosing linguistic models for my typology has been to isolate some of the minimal articulatory structures behind more visibly ideological interpretive strategies. Through a formal categorization of these structures, I have tried to eschew some of the impediments to critical agreement that are endemic to sociological, historical, biographical, psychoanalytic, and deconstructionist approaches to literature. The pertinence of strictly linguistic criteria has thereby outweighed that of any other kind in my description of the critical act.

* * *

> ... to go beyond formalism is as yet too hard for us and
> may even be [...] against the nature of understanding.[6]
> —G. Hartman

This essay began with the simple observation that critics pick out repetitions of many different varieties in a text so as to justify their respective interpretive stances. In constructing a preliminary typology of forms of iteration, my goal was to arrive at a more systematic, albeit reductive description with which to account for literariness.[7] Having completed this inexhaustive classification in representative works, we now possess a set of fundamental categories of repetitive formal features. Equipped with this new descriptive tool we can envisage future studies that would attack the whole problem of style from the perspective of numbers and kinds of repetitions at work in texts.[8]

In the meantime I should try to assess some of the stylistic differences among the three works analyzed herein. Irrespective of the particular forms they assumed, my examples of discursive intertextuality all pointed to the need a reader feels to relate prose poems back to other types of writing he knows. In "Les bons chiens" and "Dévotion," for example, certain discursive models (the ode and religious devotions) were copied negatively;

that is, they were converted into something they should not be. In *Poisson soluble* no. 1, on the contrary, the genre of the fantastic was respected more or less faithfully. The rule of prose poem functioning they manifested can thus be described as a kind of elementary law of the literary phenomenon itself: every text is read in conjunction with, or in reference to, other texts. Failing the requisite competence in literary genres or fixed forms, one risks missing the primary dimension of poeticity, discursive.

This first type of repetition is important then because, although I did not always bring it up when speaking about a specific poem, it was always the basic condition that allowed me to observe still subtler repetitive aspects. In order for me to have understood and appreciated the role of lexical repetition in Baudelaire's "Le Port," for instance, it was crucial to have established that the text copied the form of a contemplation. Had that not been understood, I might have read it as a bit of realist prose concerning a port, and ignored its repetition of the conventional depiction of death qua port. Every "true" interpretation thus presupposes at least one complete reading.[9] Without a complete reading, one cannot always perceive the discursive intertextual backdrop against which any text is written.

Below this primary level of poeticity are other features that distinguish between one text's "readability" and another's. One may have noticed in this regard that the smaller the area in which we discovered repetitions, the less we spoke of *Le Spleen de Paris*. That Baudelaire's work did not give rise in my reading to as many anagrams or other paragrammatic events as did Rimbaud's and Breton's is to be explained by the nature of its style. Though such supplementary signification may in fact be as extensive in Baudelaire as in Breton and Rimbaud, it did not impose itself into my consciousness as readily. In other words, the denotative level of the pieces in *Le Spleen de Paris* never impeded my getting some inkling of what they seemed to be expressing.

The same, however, cannot be said about the *Illuminations* or *Poisson soluble*. The less a poetic message can be received or read, therefore, as an "ordinary," i.e., non-poetic act of discourse, the more "background"[10] intratextual phenomena like anagrams come to the fore. One might argue that this qualification renders the existence of minute iterative features improbable. If they cannot be recovered from every literary text, then perhaps they are merely the consequence of a particular reader's projection. But, seeing how the perception of all stylistic features requires a certain participation on the reader's part, this argument is untenable. Just because the former demand more participation than the latter is not a reason to deny their presence.

Besides, how does one quantify reader participation? Is it really more difficult to notice anagrams than, say, phrasal intertextual repetitions? Or is it not instead the case that so-called background phenomena constitute simply a less common, less defined, and less explored area of critical study? One of the results of our analyses was precisely to translate the elusiveness of such phenomena to the reader, and to make them more common. This intrusion of unexpected strata of meaning is bound, as Anthony Johnson concludes, "to radically alter the recipient's attitude to the text and, indeed, the whole concept and practice of reading" (Johnson, p. 117).

Outside of this tendency to signal more finer and finer levels of signification (a tendency that increases from Baudelaire to Breton), the forms of our three collections resemble one another closely. Every one of their stylistic aspects could be classified in the categories we saw functioning across auctorial boundaries. While Baudelaire's style seems to depend more on the "higher" levels of iteration than did either Rimbaud's or Breton's, that does not mean that certain stylistic traits in the collection of the latter two poets will not also operate on those levels. Nor does it mean that texts in *Le Spleen de Paris* lack the semiotic potential to exhibit features from the "lower" levels. It simply suggests that any stylistic comparison of prose poems is contingent on the degree of pressure they put on the reader to descend deeper into their "boiling depths."

Being a function of a text's readability, this "pressure" represents the strength with which paragrammatic events emerge over the threshold of consciousness (Johnson, p. 114). If a syllabic repetition, for instance, does not reach our awareness, then there is no pressure to see it. But in order for it to reach our awareness in the first place, the intelligibility of the textual forms which contain it must somehow be problematic. The reader must feel that the text is expressing something more than what the words alone express. Usually, this supplement comes from an intertextual model that one is obliged to recover.

On other occasions, though, the model is idiosyncratic, and must first be found within the text's own margins. Hence, a larger proportion of intratextual repetitions in the prose poems of Rimbaud and Breton is what ultimately distinguishes them from those of Baudelaire. Rimbaud's main reproach of Baudelaire, we remember, was that he lived in too artistic a milieu.[11] From our point of view, Baudelaire's texts therefore owed too much on the surface (on a first reading or writing) to forms used by other writers. They did not assume forms that for Rimbaud were sufficiently new to accommodate the truly new that prose poems represented.[12]

In accordance with our findings, some of our earlier assumptions and provisional definitions now need to be modified. The following questions, which repeatedly threatened to divert me from my taxonomic enterprise, can finally be treated at some length: 1) What exactly is a prose poem?, 2) What relationship exists among multiple readings of a text?, and 3) How does semiotics deal with poeticity? This final section will be divided into three parts that provide some answers to these questions.

The Prose Poem

The 1916 preface to Max Jacob's prose poem collection, *Le Cornet à Dés*, states that " . . . le poème en prose pour exister doit se soumettre aux lois de tout art, qui sont le style ou la volonté et la situation ou émotion. . . ."[13] While Jacob never really explains these two laws, except abstractly, it is noteworthy that he posits this structural similarity between the prose poem and all other genres. From the beginning of my reading, I, too, assumed that prose poems were literary forms, even though at the time of my initial assumption I had a simpler reason to think so. The reason was that they are accepted as such. In a sense then, my entire essay has aimed at isolating the minimal criteria of this "as such," of literariness.

Seeing that no rules existed to govern the production of prose poems, and that readers have classified the latter within the category of literature, this type of artifact was thus presumed to be the best object in which to locate various areas of potential literary functioning. Beyond all else, the classification of repetitions is a means to identify those formal dimensions of a text that prompt a reader, in the course of his reading, to label it "literary." If there were nothing about the prose poem that transformed it in this way, superficially, one could not distinguish it from a random piece of prose.

An important switch in perspective therefore needs to be made, especially in the wake of Max Jacob's remark, "Une page en prose n'est pas un poème en prose, quand bien même elle encadrerait deux ou trois trouvailles."[14] The switch I refer to is the one from text to reader, which the prose poem, more than any *marked* genre, forces us to come to grips with. Without this change of focus, it would be entirely possible to consider any collection of words whatsoever a prose poem.[15] After all, which preestablished poetic norms would they violate?

By displacing the source of recognizable literary signs from the object under investigation to an arbiter (reader) who decides which, if any, of such signs are actually operative, i.e., pertinent, the prose poem underlines the indissociability of readers and texts. If, in an extreme case, a person had *no* previous knowledge of literature, he obviously would not know what there was about a prose poem that was "literary." It goes without saying, however, that he would be equally ignorant of such features in any other text as well. Readers who harbor a belief in a fixed notion of literature thus necessarily bring a modicum of *literary* competence to their reading. Thanks to their past experiences with poetic works, the formal peculiarities of prose poems inevitably remind readers of those found in "normal" artistic works, in which such features are de rigueur.

To the extent that prose poems take their distance from conventional literary genres, and oblige us to examine more carefully their idiolectic shapes, they manifest Jakobson's "poetic function" in exemplary fashion. Because the poetic function of language draws a reader's attention to the specific form of a message, ironically enough, prose poems are more "poetic" than standard verse. Lacking well-defined models to imitate, they make it incumbent upon the reader to synthesize poeticity (not receive it readymade) from his own personal appraisal of the signifiers on the page. This appraisal is moreover bound to involve comparison with the stock devices of other examples of verbal arts. So the less a text appears at first glance to be literary in terms of conventional practice, the more it demands the reader's active participation to help supply its missing links with literary tradition.[16]

Little wonder then that Michael Benedikt sees in the prose poem a different version of poetry: "it is a genre of poetry, self-consciously written in prose, and characterized by the intense use of virtually all the devices of poetry, which includes the intense use of devices of verse. . . ."[17] Eminently aware of literary tradition, he and other critics make the prose poem into a new "genre" where there was none before. As has already been demonstrated, this type of text does, of course, repeat aspects found elsewhere in literature. But it is equally true that part of its nature consists in rejecting earlier devices:

> il y a *à la fois* dans le poème en prose une force anarchique, destructrice, qui porte à nier les formes existantes, et une force organisatrice, qui tend à construire un "tout" poétique; et le terme même de *poème en prose* souligne cette dualité: qui écrit en prose se révolte contre les conventions métriques et stylistiques; qui écrit un poème vise à créer une forme organisée, fermée sur soi . . .[18]

From this angle, the prose poem can be regarded as the limit of literature itself. I shall define it as any short[19] text which, by dint of transgressing the canons of accepted literary discourses, borders on a non-literary or "para-literary" discourse.[20] As such, it makes the reader's burden heavier than it is when he is faced with a specific instance of a genre antedating that instance. The prose poem projects the reader "downward" as it were from the discursive level into the text's finer levels in search of the repetitions he wants so desperately for his commentary. Characterized not so much by an absence of literary devices as by a conspicuously antagonistic[21] relationship with them, it subverts the supposedly stable domain of the literary, and shows the latter to be so many moments in the history of prescriptive aesthetics: "le poème en prose est une répétition de la poésie, à travers laquelle la poésie se différencie rétrospectivement d'elle-même."[22]

The prose poem thereby devalues earlier attempts to describe and categorize earlier literary texts by exposing the transitoriness, even arbitrariness, of the concept of literary genre. It calls into question the belief that other genres represent universally agreed upon sign-posts by which a work enters into a relationship with the world of literature. It forces us to ask ourselves whether there can be one, and only one definition of genre. For as Paul Hernadi aptly points out, "the finest generic classifications of our time make us look beyond their immediate concern and focus on the *order of literature*, not on *borders between literary genres.*"[23]

At the same time, the prose poem signals the immobility or independence of literari*ness*. Although texts worthy of literary status vary according to the time and society in which they are written, their capacity to call attention to their form is what ultimately ties them together.[24] As a result, the various literary reference points or models they bring into relief become the actual basis for the qualification "literary," or lack thereof. They are what assures the literary status of prose poems. Insofar as this kind of writing is *like* literature then, it exhibits literariness.[25]

Since the above models were at one time copies, a literary text is thus an arbitrary concept, arbitrary as in the Saussurean notion of the signifier itself. It signifies "literature" only in relation to other pure differences, i.e., literary texts, in the continuum of literature. On the basis of the present study, at least, exclusion of certain written works from this continuum cannot be wholly justified by some consistent structural notion of literature, or of some "discours littéraire homogène."[26] That is because many non-literary works also exhibit the kind of formal iterability that we have tried to describe in detail here. The most we can say about the literary / non-literary distinction is that this division would still appear to be essentially a societal and conventional one. The prose poem's real specificity, therefore, lies in its driving home these points to the reader, in its formal playing with such cherished traditions.

Reading vs. Interpretation

Empirically speaking, there are two major types of reading that individuals engage in when confronted with a text. Either they read it once through and put it aside, or else they repeat their reading in order to interpret, comment on, or better understand certain parts.[27] To this first type I give the actual name *reading*; to the second, *interpretation*. On his initial reading of a text, an individual is presented with each and every textual element in a particular order, and must assimilate them accordingly. In later readings, though, he often selects not only which textual items are problematic, but also the sequence he will read them in. My intention in using these terms is to indicate the profound perceptual modification which occurs upon repeated readings.

Now some may scoff at this division on the grounds that any true reading is necessarily a rereading. For his part, Barthes insists that multiple readings of a text are the only means to save it from repetition.[28] The repetition he speaks of corresponds to what we have been calling the intertextual repetition of certain set forms that a given text copies. A single reading for Barthes thus provides clues of what the work resembles, and only informs him of what he already knows. In other words, the first time through a text yields informational units one is often familiar with from one's knowledge of a given language and literature. The reader's possession of both linguistic and literary competence permits him to recognize several syntactic and narrative patterns that, metaphorically, derive from the same story or, as referred to in our first chapter, the same Book.[29]

Far from being the text's sole salvation, however, a second or third reading should not be thought of as any "truer" than the first. As Wolfgang Iser insists, "they are, quite simply, different."[30] Yet, knowing that difference is what makes any repetition possible, I submit that with each new reading one thing never changes: there is always a mental production, or more precisely, reconstruction, of signifieds. Considering my earlier reticence to prefer a vague notion like a "signified" over the fixity of forms, this proposition undoubtedly seems to undermine much of what has been said until now. But such is not the case when we realize that no signified exists without a signifier, and that signifiers or forms are precisely what vary from reading to reading. The reason so many dissimilar "meanings" are obtained from each new interpretation of a work is that every critic takes into account a dissimilar set of forms. This is merely another way of saying that with each new reading, certain readers stress aspects that others may not have found to be of any interest.

Whether one actually has the right to proceed in such an ostensibly subjective manner when analyzing a text is, of course, the big problem that hermeneutics must resolve. If, for example, I discover an intimate connection between *Poisson soluble* no. 7 and Arthurian legend, do I then have the right to overlook the mention of Incas in the opening paragraph? The answer is both yes and no. Yes, because in my particular interpretation, every single textual element might not have been relevant to the larger (or smaller) points I was trying to make about the text. Provided that the "relevant" elements outweigh the irrelevant ones, one can, and often does, reject them for the purposes of a given argument. The critic (or "third party" alluded to in chapter one) thus always has the final say about the signified he believes needs explanation.

When, on the other hand, one reads as if everyone agreed on the important aspects of a work, one assumes that everything about a text is meant to be read in reference to the sociolect, that great body of collective knowledge we all share. For this kind of critic, the answer to the above question is no. For him, the Incas in Breton's prose poem would have to be explained in terms of their intertextual relationship with King Arthur. This can be done easily enough, however, if one sees in that signifier another sign of a much earlier, exotic, and almost legendary group of people. From this semiotic perspective, *Incas* would be just one more index of some *other* time period and society that the text points to more specifically on other formal levels.

Were everyone to delimit a text in exactly the same manner, therefore, the context within which he perceived a meaning would remain constant. Presumably, an interpretive consensus could be expected more frequently than actually happens. As gratifying to students, teachers, and critics as that might be, one can never divide a text into smaller or larger units (*lexies*)[31] except at the risk of turning the whole segmentation process into a supremely arbitrary,[32] imminently authoritarian operation. The context afforded by a specific choice of signifiers conditions, to a very large extent, the meaning(s) one might derive from it. And whenever a sentence or group of words contains no apparent sense, there always seems to be someone who can come up with an appropriate frame that *makes* it signify.[33]

The upshot of these remarks is this: while meaning is context-bound, the point at which a specific stylistic context begins, and where meaning is apprehended, depends on the reader, especially on his memory and attention.[34] The reader perceives an uninterrupted series of textual forms that, in principle, adds to everything he and the writer have already brought to, or along with (*con-textus*) the text. The "rereader" or critic, on the other hand, decides when and where these potentially infinite intertexts begin. If I had not remembered or paid attention to the initial phrasal intertextual repetition in *Poisson soluble* no. 7, for example, the stylistic context in which I read, "ils lancent le merveilleux lasso," might have begun instead with the word, "Incas." In that case, I would have been hard-pressed to infer the anagram that otherwise stood out clearly in a medieval context.

As the critic is the one who ultimately determines what is pertinent to his interpretation, it is thus important for us to recognize the following situation of hermeneutics: meaning depends on context, while context depends on a specific set of contextual limits. These limits are both intrinsic and extrinsic to a text. Its intrinsic limit is provided by the totality of signifiers which makes up the entire text, something only readers respect. Critics, for their part, substitute their extrinsic choices—even though they are not always conscious of them—for the letter of the text. They seem to prefer them to the theoretically irreducible, indivisible whole of the work. The choices they make are what divides the text into segments that are, first and foremost, comprehensible to them. These same choices define the way a narrative is put together by the particular analyst.[35]

But the printed text, in all its materiality, does not need to be segmented, conceptualized, or otherwise symbolized, in order to exist in the world. Quoting once again from Barthes: "Lire, c'est désirer l'oeuvre, c'est vouloir être l'oeuvre, c'est refuser de doubler l'oeuvre en dehors de toute autre parole que la parole même de l'oeuvre [. . .] Passer de la lecture à la critique, c'est changer de désir, c'est désirer non plus l'oeuvre, mais son propre langage."[36] According to Barthes, the solitary commentary that a true reader can make is a pastiche of the work under examination. By staying close to the letter of the text, one can avoid confusing what really belongs to the writer's style with what one would have belong to it. Outside of copying it verbatim, however, this procedure will inevitably lead to certain suggested revisions or modifications which, in their turn, become as suspect as any would-be interpretation. So one either talks about certain finite aspects of texts, i.e., produces an interpretation, or else one just reads them. Whenever one interprets, one has already necessarily reread,[37] which means simply that a myriad of mental operations occur whose purpose is to juxtapose textual elements with those of one's linguistic and literary competence. This hermeneutic process makes "sense" of a text.[38]

Moreover, any bringing together of an inside (the text) and the outside (the intertext) is what any work is "about." Since it intertextually repeats many attested units of a sociolect, a text is about that which it describes, represents, or states.[39] But, by the same token, a text also just *is*. Understood as an ordinary act of communication, it obviously must be about something previously established. As literature, though, it must also be thought of as a unique utterance that can tolerate no metalinguistic elucidation. There can be no other critical justification for its assuming a specific form to the exclusion of any other.

If the statement, "this text just *is*," does not satisfy a given reader he perforce turns to an analysis of the work's idiolectic features. He then rereads, becomes a critic, and begins to rewrite. Whenever that happens, however, repetition returns as the epistemological foundation of his commentary. The models permitting him to say what those features are "about" are merely displaced from the outside to the inside. Thus, intratextual features should first be thought of as being about other intratextual features, before they are compared to intertextual models they are later recognized to repeat.

In this light, my typology would name the moments in any interpretation when some type of formal repetition is seen to take place. The passage of reading to criticism manifests itself as an orderly telescoping of focus (or descent in our iterative hierarchy) from the discursive level to the paragrammatic.[40] In other words, simultaneous with our commenting on a text is our recognition of its genre, and echoes of clichés, stereotypes, and the rest. With every new perusal of the work, this progression of course does not have to be duplicated. The reader-turned-critic has no need to keep telling himself that a text is a novel, or that one of its phrases is a copy of a famous phrase, in order for him to be able to skip around to other levels and discover subtler, though still significant, repetitive traits.

One can suppose nevertheless that during the critic's earlier reading several intertextual connections were at least made unconsciously. These were subsequently amalgamated into an enlarged stylistic context in which, and with which, he works. As each additional revelation gives him the incentive to explore other areas of a work's poeticity, he may well end up examining aspects, e.g., accent marks, that few others would bother taking seriously. On the condition that his results be consistent with signifieds he deduces from the work, they will oblige him to consider these relatively unknown textual dimensions all the more carefully upon later readings. In this fashion, interpretation suddenly turns into a pioneering activity, one that is more concerned with our developing responses to the marks on the page than with our previous responses.[41] The more one learns about a given piece of literature, the more one tends to look for similar stylistic features in other works. Intertextual confirmation is therefore the final guarantor of the verisimilitude of an intratextual feature.

Semiotic Analyses of Poeticity

According to C. S. Peirce, a sign is "something knowing which we know something more."[42] In view of this, semiotics would be society's most sophisticated method to attribute a meta-language to the literary text (a set of signs). By definition, this other text is not the work. As a critical tool, it would play an intermediary role between a text's idiolect and the sociolect which grounds that very meta-language. But since only a text's graphemes (and not necessarily the public's perception of them) remain stable throughout time, these two poles of the hermeneutic phenomenon do not function uniformly. Critics from the same culture, though they may hold in common an enormous amount of literary and other linguistic material, do not always stress the same things. Because of their economic, psychological, even physiological heterogeneity, they frequently eschew certain aspects of their sociolect in order to emphasize others.[43] Thus, while it is many a semiotician's goal to be objective in his studies, he can never totally escape a certain subjectivity. If the repetition of signs guides even the best of critics through their rereadings, then there is no legitimate reason *a priori* to isolate some to the exclusion of others.

Working hypotheses are consequently the necessary conditions for the choices one makes during one's analysis of a literary work. Without such principles, any given critical stance would be on very shaky turf indeed. One would not be able to know, for instance, exactly why one's reading was better than someone else's. Yet, as Johathan Culler suggests, "the theory of the sign [semiotics] leads to theoretical principles which must be *repressed* if analysis is to take place . . ." (my emphasis).[44] One cannot, that is, waste all of one's time contemplating the ultimate signified of a signifier, for the simple reason that the former forever recedes in the kind of infinite regress most deconstructive reading ends up pursuing. Instead, one has to draw the line somewhere, and decide when a central idea like *signifiers refer only to other signifiers* needs to be strategically forgotten. If I say that prose poems are literary because of their close relationships to literature, I must temporarily repress the fact that I still do not know what literature (itself a "pure" difference) is. My analysis of prose poems might otherwise never get underway, or might never end.

Hence, the social, conventional character of a given semiotic approach to literature has to be assumed before it can work. For my interpretation to be convincing, my audience must be sufficiently satisfied with the models I claim are repeated by specific copies. If my models (the "something more" in Peirce's definition) are not well-known to my audience, one might believe that the copies I find are not signs at all. The critic who dwells too long on his theoretical stance, therefore, will often not be able to move on to his actual analysis.

Does this imply that one should discard or so distort the concept of poeticity that the semiotician could claim anything he wished to about the signs and corresponding signifying mechanisms of a literary text? Should what has been described as a "laissez-faire field, a free for all"[45] be left to readers? Because paragrammatic textual phenomena, for instance, lie outside of any codified tradition, could it not be argued that, as such, they are actually not signs at all? The answer to these rhetorical questions is negative. In every critical act the individual has to construct, or more precisely, re-construct, what he takes to be certain unsaid, inexplicit aspects of the poetic work. This has little to do with intentionality. The fact is that a text's poeticity is simply not self-explanatory; it needs an observer who can locate and describe it. The "something more" a sign lets us know does not have to be a constant value (e.g., a denotation) that we always find associated with it in the sociolect. It may instead be peculiar to, or idiolectic within, a context that the poem itself creates.

Seeing then that many linguistic signs belong only to the message (*parole*), not just the code (*langue*), we obviously have to distinguish between an utterance and the critical usage to which it may be put.[46] While a series of utterances, a text, can indeed be said to signify in relation to the code, this does not preclude its instituting a code of its own. Thus, even though Baudelaire's "Le Mauvais Vitrier" signifies in reference to an established cliché for a scandal, it also develops its own narrative grammar, based on the words "casser les vitres" *by themselves*, considered from outside of that convention.

I am now in a position to qualify Lotman's remark quoted in the first chapter of this essay. Reducing all artistic construction to repetition may very well *appear* erroneous, as he said, but when it comes down to a text's stylistic features, there seems to be no other method available to describe them. As long as critics speak about literature, they will continue to isolate its forms. These forms, in their turn, will be understood only in terms of models a particular analyst first has to recover. In this way, literary forms are caught within a symbolic realm that functions on the epistemological ground of repetition.

As a modern descendant of Russian Formalism, therefore, semiotics cannot hope to be the "self-consistent discourse of a science but [will instead always be] a *text*"[47] in its own right. If semioticians, as well as most other literary critics, cannot somehow alter the practice of their science, they will never break out of the enlarged text that their interpretation superimposes onto a nowhere-present, originary text. This text—but which text?—is the one they will have always attempted to interpret *objectively*.

NOTES

[1]This is Kristéva's original term for the now sometimes banalized notion of "intertextuality." See *La Révolution du langage poétique*, p. 59ff.

[2]For a fascinating modern study of this shield and of its narrative pertinence, see Françoise Létoublon's article entitled "Le Miroir et la boucle," *Poétique*, 53 (1983), 19-36.

[3]This analysis would be similar to the one we performed on texts 21 and 22 of Breton's *Poisson soluble*.

[4]As does Jean Milly in his *La Phrase de Proust* (Paris: Larousse, 1975), p. 10.

[5]Johnson, "Anagrammatism in Poetry," pp. 92-98.

[6]Geoffrey Hartman, *Beyond Formalism* (New Haven: Yale University Press, 1971), p. 42.

[7]It is systematic in that repetition acts as the basis for each category. But it is also reductive insofar as it considers all differences to be phenomenal instances that are understood solely in terms of repeated paradigms. A repeated paradigm or *concept* (Deleuze's word) which would subsume x and y, for example, is what permits us to say that they are different. In this case, one possible paradigm is that of *letters*.

[8]This would make them similar to Rastier's "stylistique des isotopies" proposed in François Rastier, *Essais de sémiotique poétique* (Paris: Larousse, 1972), p. 83.

[9]Cf. Roland Barthes's comment, "ceux qui négligent de relire s'obligent à lire partout la même histoire" in *S / Z (* (Paris: Seuil, 1970), pp. 22-3. What Barthes means by this is that the first reading only gives us an idea of what a text is *like*, not of what it *is* as a separate and distinct scriptural artifact.

[10]Cf. Anthony Johnson, "Anagrammatism in Poetry," p. 114. The next two quotations are from this same article.

[11]In Rimbaud's letter to Paul Démeny in his *Oeuvres*, ed. Bernard, p. 349.

[12]Cf. Rimbaud's remark, "les inventions d'inconnu réclament des formes nouvelles." *Ibid*.

[13]Max Jacob, *Le Cornet à Dés*, p. 17.

[14]*Ibid*.

[15]This is precisely what the Surrealists and Dadaists seem to be suggesting. See Breton's *Manifestes du Surréalisme*, pp. 49-52.

[16]See Riffaterre's comments on this idea in *Semiotics of Poetry*, p. 124.

[17]Michael Benedikt, *The Prose Poem* (New York: Dell, 1976), p. 47.

[18]Suzanne Bernard, *Le Poème en prose de Baudelaire jusqu'à nos jours*, p. 444.

[19]This makes the formal criterion of brevity an important stylistic component of the prose poem. Michel Beaujour argues for this same point in his article "Short Epiphanies: Two Contextual Approaches to the French Prose Poem," in *The Prose Poem in France*, ed. Mary Ann Caws and Hermine Riffaterre (New York: Columbia University Press, 1983), pp. 40-49.

[20]In an important footnote (no. 2, p. 55, *La Production du texte*), Riffaterre alludes to the possibility of such genres, but appears reluctant to pursue the point. Would para-literature undermine the entire class of literary texts? Also see *Entretiens sur la Paralittérature* with Noel Arnaud, Francis Lacassin and Jean Tortel (Paris: Librairie Plon, 1970), especially pp. 9-31.

[21]I say "antagonistic" because it struggles with them, fights against them. Instead of assuming a preestablished metrical form, for example, *Poisson soluble* no. 3 presents a series of phonemes, spread out irregularly along the first paragraph, which "rhymes" with the key word, *question*.

[22]Barbara Johnson, "Quelques différences anatomiques," p. 465.

[23]Paul Hernadi, *Beyond Genre* (Ithaca, N.Y.: Cornell University Press, 1972), p. 184.

[24]Jakobson clarifies this point in his *Questions de poétique* (Paris: Seuil, 1973), pp. 123-4.

[25]And just because they were not thought of as "proper" literature at first does not mean they did not always have the potential to illustrate the poetic function. The proof is that in our century they have drawn attention to themselves in a massive way, from both poets and critics.

[26]Tzvetan Todorov, *Les Genres du discours* (Paris: Seuil, 1978), p. 25.

[27]Barthes makes an analogous distinction in *Le Plaisir du texte* (Paris: Seuil, 1973), pp. 22-24.

[28]Roland Barthes, *S/Z*, pp. 22-3.

[29]For Gerald Prince's "zero-degree narratee" there is no such Book. Our reader is thus more like Fish's idealized reader. The two constructs are defined, respectively, in Prince, "Introduction to the Study of the Narratee" in *Reader-Response Criticism: From Formalism to Post-Structuralism*, pp. 10-11; and in Stanley Fish, *Self-Consuming Artifacts* (Berkeley: University of California Press, 1972), p. 406.

[30]Wolfgang Iser, "The Reading Process: A Phenomenological Approach" in *Reader-Response Criticism: From Formalism to Post-Structuralism*, p. 56.

[31]Barthes, *S/Z*, p. 20.

[32]*S / Z*, p. 24: "Ce découpage, il faut le dire, sera on ne peut plus arbitraire."

[33]This is my paraphrase of Jonathan Culler from his "Convention and Meaning: Derrida and Austin," *New Literary History*, Vol. XIII, No. 1 (Autumn 1981), 23.

[34]Riffaterre, *Essais de stylistique structurale*, p. 81.

[35]Cf. Holland, *5 Readers Reading*, p. 39: "the way one puts a story together derives from the patterns and structures in the mind one brings to the story."

[36]Roland Barthes, *Critique et Vérité* (Paris: Seuil, 1966), p. 79.

[37]Cf. the very first line of B. Johnson's *The Critical Difference*, which reads as follows: "Literary criticism as such can perhaps best be called the art of rereading."

[38]N. Holland, alluding to Freud, claims that this process represents the way the mind itself works when dealing with any aspect of reality. See his *5 Readers Reading*, p. 14.

[39]This is contrary to Paul de Man's opinion as expressed in his *Allegories of Reading* (New Haven: Yale University Press, 1979), p. 57.

[40]Philippe Sollers gives a similar picture of the critic's decoding procedure in his "Niveaux sémantiques d'un texte moderne" in *Théorie d'ensemble* (Paris: Seuil, 1968), p. 324. However, his description is aimed exclusively at modern texts and does not appear to have a larger application.

[41]This is how Fish describes his critical method in "Affective Stylistics," p. 404.

[42]*Collected Papers*, the letter to Lady Welby of 12 October 1904.

[43]In her poetic analyses, Kristéva, for instance, will attach great importance to the repetitions of a language's phonemes, whereas Riffaterre prefers those of more codified semantic elements.

[44]Jonathan Culler, "Semiotics and Deconstruction," *Poetics Today*, 1, No. 1-2 (Autumn 1979), 141.

[45]Benjamin Hrushovski, "The Meaning of Sound Patterns in Poetry: An Interaction Theory," *Poetics Today*, 2, No. la (1980), 55.

[46]Linda Waugh, "The Poetic Function in the Theory of Roman Jakobson," p. 62.

[47]Jonathan Culler, "Semiotics and Deconstruction," p. 141.

APPENDIX A

LE PELERINAGE DE SAINTE-ANNE

Saint-Pol Roux

Les cinq Gars de faïence, à la peau de falaise, aux yeux couleur d'océan qui s'apaise, vont, bras dessus, vers la chapelle peinte où, vieillement jolie, sourit la bonne Sainte.

Mises dimanchement, emparfumées de marjolaine, bras dessous les accompagnent les cinq Promises de porcelaine mignonnes comme des joujoux et dont la joue rayonne ainsi qu'une pomme d'api,—car ils reviennent des baleines, des lugubres baleines aux vilaines bouches, les salubres marins destinés à leurs couches.

Donc la guirlande juvénile vers Sainte-Anne marche, à travers la lande puérile, les lins et les moulins, les ruches, le blé noir, les meules, les manoirs, les clochers de pain bis, les vaches, les brebis, et les chèvres bêlant à la manière des aïeules.

Et, l'âme vive, l'on arrive à la chapelle peinte où, vieillement jolie, sourit la bonne Sainte.

Viennent offrir, les fils des vagues, leur offrande viennent offrir à la Marraine aux fins yeux d'algue, à la Marraine des marins, qui, les sauvant des loups gloutons du vent noroît, guida leurs grands moutons de bois vers le bercail de Cornouailles.

Et les voici cerchant au tréfonds de leurs poches, sous le bonjour des cloches, et les voici cherchant le Coeur d'or ou d'argent juré devant l'écueil qui peinturlure en deuil les femmes de futaine allant pleurer à la fontaine . . .

Et les voilà cherchant le Coeur d'or ou d'argent, cependant que sur l'herbe et la mousse, lassées par la route, elles s'étendent toutes, les douces fiancées aux longs cheveux de gerbe.

Mais ils ne trouvent dans leurs poches, sous le bonjour des cloches, ne trouvent que des sous, du corail, de l'amadou, puis des médailles; les Coeurs d'or ou d'argent nullement.

Surpris, et pâles plus que des surplus, aussitôt, ils comprennent qu'ils oublièrent au village l'ex-voto.

Lors pleurent les marins, dociles pèlerins, qui point ne veulent faire veuve des cadeaux la Sainte aux fins yeux d'algue envoyant des radeaux aux voyages fragiles,—tant on devient pieux d'aller par la mer bleue sous la superbe croix du mât et de la vergue!

Dans la brise, tout bas, déjà dorment les Promises de porcelaine emparfumées de marjolaine.

* * *

Tout à coup, dressant le cou, les cinq Gars de faïence tirent de leur ceinture cinq couteaux plus brillants que cinq sardines de Lorient et se dirigent, sur l'orteil, vers les cinq vierges en sommeil.

Les oreilles d'icelles, emmi les tresses blondes, semblent des coquillages dans le sable de l'onde.

Comme pour faire des folies, les cinq Gars s'agenouillent devant les Jolies rêvant sur l'herbe verte ainsi qu'est verte une grenouille.

Lorsqu'a défait chaque jeune homme corsage et corselet où rient deux pommes de Quimperlé, voici qu'en les poitrines vives ils font d'un geste preste, avec des yeux de chandelier, font s'enfoncer les sardines d'acier.

Giclant soudain, du rose arrose la frimousse des anciens mousses. On dirait qu'un rosier de forge les pavoise d'un reflet, ou qu'ils mangèrent, jusqu'à la gorge et le gosier, des mûres et des framboises.

Leurs mains plongent enfin dans les poitrines belles et retirent cinq Coeurs, cinq Coeurs battant de l'aile.

Dans la brise, toujours dorment les Promises de porcelaine emparfumées de marjolaine.

Ensuite, ayant cousu les chairs—avec le fil du baiser cher en l'aiguille des dents—et refermé corsages, corselets où rient deux pommes de Quimperlé, les cinq Gars de faïence entrent dans la chapelle peinte offrir les Coeurs, les Coeurs battant de l'aile, à la Sainte aux fins yeux d'algue qui, les sauvant des loups gloutons du vent noroît, guida leurs grands moutons de bois vers le bercail de Cornouailles.

* * *

Hélas! quand ils sortirent devers la mousse et l'herbe, plus ne virent leurs Douces aux longs cheveux de gerbe.

Toutes là-bas partaient, partaient parmi la route qui blanche, se déroule jusqu'au village où l'on roucoule.

Eux les appellent par leurs noms: Yvonne, Marthe, Marion, Naïc et Madeleine!

Mais point ne se tournent les belles, Yvonne, Marthe, Marion, Naïc et Madeleine; et les vilaines au loin s'en vont.

Si loin que leur coiffelette, d'abord aile de mouette, devient aile de papillon, puis flocon de neige fondu par l'horizon . . .

Tombent alors en défaillance les cinq Gars de faïence tandis que disparaissent les cinq Promises de porcelaine emparfumées de marjolaine.

De coeur n'ayant plus, elles n'aimaient plus: Yvonne, Marthe, Marion, Naïc et Madeleine.

APPENDIX B

POISSON SOLUBLE no. 1

André Breton

Le parc, à cette heure, étendait ses mains blondes au-dessus de la fontaine magique. Un château sans signification roulait à la surface de la terre. Près de Dieu le cahier de ce château était ouvert sur un dessin d'ombres, de plumes, d'iris. Au Baiser de la jeune Veuve, c'était le nom de l'auberge caressée par la vitesse de l'automobile et par les suspensions d'herbes horizontales. Aussi jamais les branches datées de l'année précédente ne remuaient à l'approche des stores, quand la lumière précipite les femmes au balcon. La jeune Irlandaise troublée par les jérémiades du vent d'est écoutait dans son sein rire les oiseaux de mer.

"Filles du sépulcre bleu, jours de fête, formes sonnées de l'angélus de mes yeux et de ma tête quand je m'éveille, usages des provinces flammées, vous m'apportez le soleil des menuiseries blanches, des scieries mécaniques et du vin. C'est mon ange pâle, mes mains si rassurées. Mouettes du paradis perdu!"

Le fantôme entre sur la pointe des pieds. Il inspecte rapidement la tour et descend l'escalier triangulaire. Ses bas de soie rouge jettent une lueur tournoyante sur les coteaux de jonc. Le fantôme a environ deux cents ans, il parle encore un peu français. Mais dans sa chair transparente se conjuguent la rosée du soir et la sueur des astres. Il est perdu pour lui-même en cette contrée attendrie. L'orme mort et le très vert catalpa sont seuls à soupirer dans l'avalanche de lait des etoiles farouches. Un noyau éclate dans un fruit. Puis le poissonnacelle passe, les mains sur ses yeux, demandant des perles ou des robes.

Une femme chante à la fenêtre de ce château du XIVe siècle. Dans ses rêves il y a des noyers noirs. Je ne la connais pas encore parce que le fantôme fait trop le beau temps autour de lui. La nuit est venue tout d'un coup comme une grande rosace de fleurs retournée sur nos têtes.

Un bâtiment est la cloche de nos fuites: la fuite à cinq heures du matin, lorsque la pâleur assaille les belles voyageuses du rapide dans leur lit de fougère, la fuite à une heure de l'après-midi en passant par l'olive du meurtre. Un bâtiment est la cloche de nos fuites dans une église pareille à l'ombre de Mme de Pompadour. Mais je sonnais à la grille du château.

A ma rencontre vinrent plusieurs servantes vêtues d'une combinaison collante de satin couleur du jour. Dans la nuit démente, leurs visages apitoyés témoignaient de la peur d'être compromises. "Vous désirez?

—Dites à votre maîtresse que le bord de son lit est une rivière de fleurs. Ramenez-la dans ce caveau de théâtre où battait à l'envi, il y a trois ans, le coeur d'une capitale que j'ai oubliée. Dites-lui que son temps m'est précieux et que dans le chandelier de ma tête flambent toutes ses rêveries. N'oubliez pas de lui faire part de mes désirs couvant sous les pierres que vous êtes. Et toi qui es plus belle qu'une graine de soleil dans le bec du perroquet éblouissant de cette porte, dis-moi tout de suite comment elle se porte. S'il est vrai que le pont-levis des lierres de la parole s'abaisse ici sur un simple appel d'étrier.

—Tu as raison, me dit-elle, l'ombre ici présente est sortie tantôt à cheval. Les guides étaient faites de mots d'amour, je crois, mais puisque les naseaux du brouillard et les sachets d'azur t'ont conduit à cette porte éternellement battante, entre et caresse-moi tout le long de ces marches semées de pensées."

De bas en haut s'envolaient de grandes guêpes isocèles. La jolie aurore du soir me précédait, les yeux au ciel de mes yeux sans se retourner. Ainsi les navires se couchent dans la tempête d'argent.

Plusieurs échos se répondent sur terre : l'écho des pluies comme le bouchon d'une ligne, l'écho du soleil comme la soude mêlée au sable. L'écho présent est celui des larmes, et de la beauté propre aux aventures illisibles, aux rêves tronqués. Nous arrivions à destination. Le fantôme, qui, en chemin, s'était avisé de faire corps avec saint Denis, prétendait voir dans chaque rose sa tête coupée. Un balbutiement collé aux vitres et à la rampe, balbutiement froid, se joignait à nos baisers sans retenue.

Sur le bord des nuages se tient une femme, sur le bord des îles une femme se tient comme sur les hauts murs décorés de vigne étincelante le raisin mûrit, à belles grappes dorées et noires. Il y a aussi le plant de vigne américain et cette femme était un plant de vigne américain, de l'espèce la plus récemment acclimatée en France et qui donne des grains de ce mauve digitale dont la pleine saveur n'a pas encore été éprouvée. Elle allait et venait dans un appartement couloir analogue aux wagons couloirs des grands express européens, à cette différence près que le rayonnement des lampes spécifiait mal les coulées de lave, les minarets et la grande paresse des bêtes de l'air et de l'eau. Je toussai plusieurs fois et le train en question glissa à travers des tunnels, endormit des ponts suspendus. La divinité du lieu chancela. L'ayant reçue dans mes bras, toute bruissante, je portai mes lèvres à sa gorge sans mot dire. Ce qui se passe ensuite m'échappe presque entièrement. Je ne nous retrouve que plus tard, elle dans une toilette terriblement vive qui la fait ressembler à un engrenage dans une machine toute neuve, moi terré autant que possible dans cet habit noir impeccable que depuis je ne quitte plus.

J'ai dû passer, entre-temps, par un cabaret tenu par des ligueurs très anciens que mon état-civil plongea dans une perplexité d'oiseaux. Je me souviens aussi d'une grue élevant au ciel des paquets qui devaient être des cheveux, avec quelle effrayante légèreté, mon Dieu. Puis ce fut l'avenir, l'avenir même. L'Enfant-Flamme, la merveilleuse Vague de tout à l'heure guidait mes pas comme des guirlandes. Les craquelures du ciel me réveillèrent enfin : il n'y avait plus de parc, plus de jour ni de nuit, plus d'enterrements blancs menés par des cerceaux de verre. La femme qui se tenait près de moi mirait ses pieds dans une flaque d'eau d'hiver.

A distance je ne vois plus clair, c'est comme si une cascade s'interposait entre le théâtre de ma vie et moi, qui n'en suis pas le principal acteur. Un bourdonnement chéri m'accompagne, le long duquel les herbes jaunissent et même cassent. Quand je lui dis : "Prends ce verre fumé qui est ma main dans tes mains, voici l'éclipse" elle sourit et plonge dans les mers pour en ramener la branche de corail du sang. Nous ne sommes pas loin du pré de la mort et pourtant nous nous abritons du vent et de l'espoir dans ce salon flétri. L'aimer, j'y ai songé comme on aime. Mais la moitié d'un citron vert, ses cheveux de rame, l'étourderie des pièges à prendre les bêtes vivantes, je n'ai pu m'en défaire complètement. A présent elle dort, face à l'infini de mes amours, devant cette glace que les souffles terrestres ternissent. C'est quand elle dort qu'elle m'appartient vraiment, j'entre dans son rêve comme un voleur et je la perds vraiment comme on perd une couronne. Je suis dépossédé des racines de l'or, assurément, mais je tiens les fils de la tempête et je garde les cachets de cire du crime.

Le moindre ourlet des airs, là où fuit et meurt le faisan de la lune, là où erre le peigne éblouissant des cachots, là où trempe la jacinthe du mal, je l'ai décrit dans mes moments de lucidité de plus en plus rare, soulevant trop tendrement cette brume lointaine. Maintenant c'est la douceur qui reprend, le boulevard pareil à un marais salant sous les enseignes lumineuses. Je rapporte des fruits sauvages, des baies ensoleillées que je lui donne et qui sont entre ses mains des bijoux immenses. Il faut encore éveiller les frissons dans les broussailles de la chambre, lacer des ruisseaux dans la fenêtre du jour. Cette tâche est l'apothéose amusante de tout, qui, bien qu'on soit assez fatigué, nous tient encore en éveil, homme et femme, selon les itinéraires de la lumière dès qu'on a su la ralentir. Servantes de la faiblesse, servantes du bonheur, les femmes abusent de la lumière dans un éclat de rire.

APPENDIX C

ENFANCE

Arthur Rimbaud

I

Cette idole, yeux noirs et crin jaune, sans parents ni cour, plus noble que la fable, mexicaine et flamande; son domaine, azur et verdure insolents, court sur des plages nommées, par des vagues sans vaisseaux, de noms férocement grecs, slaves, celtiques.

A la lisière de la forêt—les fleurs de rêve tintent, éclatent, éclairent,—la fille à lèvre d'orange, les genoux croisés dans le clair déluge qui sourd des prés, nudité qu'ombrent, traversent et habillent les arcs-en-ciel, la flore, la mer.

Dames qui tournoient sur les terrasses voisines de la mer; enfantes et géantes, superbes noires dans la mousse vert-de-gris, bijoux debout sur le sol gras des bosquets et des jardinets dégelés,—jeunes mères et grandes soeurs aux regards pleins de pèlerinages, sultanes, princesses de démarche et de costume tyranniques, petites étrangères et personnes doucement malheureuses.

Quel ennui, l'heure du "cher corps" et "cher coeur."

II

C'est elle, la petite morte, derrière les rosiers.—La jeune maman trépassée descend le perron.—La calèche du cousin crie sur le sable.—Le petit frère (il est aux Indes!) là, devant le couchant, sur le pré d'oeillets.—Les vieux qu'on a enterrés tout droits dans le rempart aux giroflées.

L'essaim des feuilles d'or entoure la maison du général. Ils sont dans le midi.—On suit la route rouge pour arriver à l'auberge vide. Le château est à vendre; les persiennes sont détachées.—Le curé aura emporté la clef de l'église.—Autour du parc, les loges des gardes sont inhabitées. Les palissades sont si hautes qu'on ne voit que les cimes bruissantes. D'ailleurs il n'y a rien à voir là-dedans.

Les prés remontent aux hameaux sans coqs, sans enclumes. L'écluse est levée. O les calvaires et les moulins du désert, les îles et les meules!

Des fleurs magiques bourdonnaient. Les talus le berçaient. Des bêtes d'une élégance fabuleuse circulaient. Les nuées s'amassaient sur la haute mer faite d'une éternité de chaudes larmes.

III

Au bois il y a un oiseau, son chant vous arrête et vous fait rougir.

Il y a une horloge qui ne sonne pas.

Il y a une fondrière avec un nid de bêtes blanches.

Il y a une cathédrale qui descend et un lac qui monte.

Il y a une petite voiture abandonée dans le taillis, ou qui descend le sentier en courant, enrubannée.

Il y a une troupe de petits comédiens en costumes, aperçus sur la route à travers la lisière du bois.

Il y a enfin, quand l'on a faim et soif, quelqu'un qui vous chasse.

IV

Je suis le saint, en prière sur la terrasse,—comme les bêtes pacifiques paissent jusqu'à la mer de Palestine.

Je suis le savant au fauteuil sombre. Les branches et la pluie se jettent à la croisée de la bibliothèque.

Je suis le piéton de la grand'route par les bois nains; la rumeur des écluses couvre mes pas. Je vois longtemps la mélancolique lessive d'or du couchant.

Je serais bien l'enfant abandonné sur la jetée partie à la haute mer, le petit valet suivant l'allée dont le front touche le ciel.

Les sentiers sont âpres. Les monticules se couvrent de genêts. L'air est immobile. Que les oiseaux et les sources sont loin! Ce ne peut être que la fin du monde, en avançant.

V

Qu'on me loue enfin ce tombeau, blanchi à la chaux avec les lignes du ciment en relief—très loin sous terre.

Je m'accoude à la table, la lampe éclaire très vivement ces journaux que je suis idiot de relire, ces livres sans intérêt.—

A une distance énorme au-dessus de mon salon souterrain, les maisons s'implantent, les brunes s'assemblent. La boue est rouge ou noire. Ville monstrueuse, nuit sans fin!

Moins haut, sont des égouts. Aux côtés, rien que l'épaisseur du globe. Peut-être les gouffres d'azur, des puits de feu. C'est peut-être sur ces plans que se rencontrent lunes et comètes, mers et fables.

Aux heures d'amertume je m'imagine des boules de saphir, de métal. Je suis maître du silence. Pourquoi une apparence de soupirail blêmirait-elle au coin de la voûte?

APPENDIX D

LE JOUJOU DU PAUVRE

Charles Baudelaire

Je veux donner l'idée d'un divertissement innocent. Il y a si peu d'amusements qui ne soient pas coupables!

Quand vous sortirez le matin avec l'intention décidée de flâner sur les grandes routes, remplissez vos poches de petites inventions à un sou—telles que le polichinelle plat mû par un seul fil, les forgerons qui battent l'enclume, le cavalier et son cheval dont la queue est un sifflet,—et le long des cabarets, au pied des arbres, faites-en hommage aux enfants inconnus et pauvres que vous rencontrerez. Vous verrez leurs yeux s'agrandir démesurément. D'abord ils n'oseront pas prendre; ils douteront de leur bonheur. Puis leurs mains agripperont vivement le cadeau, et ils s'enfuiront comme font les chats qui vont manger loin de vous le morceau que vous leur avez donné, ayant appris à se défier de l'homme.

Sur une route, derrière la grille d'un vaste jardin, au bout duquel apparaissait la blancheur d'un joli château frappé par le soleil, se tenait un enfant beau et frais, habillé de ces vêtements de campagne si pleins de coquetterie.

Le luxe, l'insouciance et le spectacle habituel de la richesse, rendent ces enfants-là si jolis qu'on les croirait faits d'une autre pâte que les enfants de la médiocrité ou de la pauvreté.

A côté de lui, gisait sur l'herbe un joujou splendide, aussi frais que son maître, verni, doré, vêtu d'une robe pourpre, et couvert de plumets et de verroteries. Mais l'enfant ne s'occupait pas de son joujou préféré, et voici ce qu'il regardait:

De l'autre côté de la grille, sur la route, entre les chardons et les orties, il y avait un autre enfant, sale, chétif, fuligineux, un de ces marmots-parias dont un oeil impartial découvrirait la beauté, si, comme l'oeil du connaisseur devine une peinture idéale sous un vernis de carrossier, il le nettoyait de la répugnante patine de la misère.

A travers ces barreaux symboliques séparant deux mondes, la grande route et le château, l'enfant pauvre montrait à l'enfant riche son propre joujou, que celui-ci examinait avidement comme un objet rare et inconnu. Or, ce joujou, que le petit souillon agaçait, agitait et secouait dans une boîte grillée, c'était un rat vivant! Les parents, par économie sans doute, avaient tiré le joujou de la vie elle-même.

Et les deux enfants se riaient l'un à l'autre fraternellement, avec des dents d'une *égale* blancheur.

APPENDIX E

LA CHAMBRE DOUBLE

Charles Baudelaire

Une chambre qui ressemble à une rêverie, une chambre véritablement *spirituelle*, où l'atmosphère stagnante est légèrement teintée de rose et de bleu.

L'âme y prend un bain de paresse, aromatisé par le regret et le désir.— C'est quelque chose de crépusculaire, de bleuâtre et de rosâtre; un rêve de volupté pendant une éclipse.

Les meubles ont des formes allongées, prostrées, alanguies. Les meubles ont l'air de rêver; on les dirait loués d'une vie somnambulique, comme le végétal et le minéral. Les étoffes parlent une langue muette, comme les fleurs, comme les ciels, comme les soleils couchants.

Sur les murs nulle abomination artistique. Relativement au rêve pur, à l'impression non analysée, l'art défini, l'art positif est un blasphème. Ici, tout a la suffisante clarté et la délicieuse obscurité de l'harmonie.

Une senteur infinitésimale du choix le plus exquis, à laquelle se mêle une très légère humidité, nage dans cette atmosphère, où l'esprit sommeillant est bercé par des sensations de serre chaude.

La mousseline pleut abondamment devant les fenêtres et devant le lit; elle s'épanche en cascades neigeuses. Sur ce lit est couchée l'Idole, la souveraine des rêves. Mais comment est-elle ici? Qui l'a amenée? quel pouvoir magique l'a installée sur ce trône de rêverie et de volupté? Qu'importe? la voilà! je la reconnais.

Voilà bien ces yeux dont la flamme traverse le crépuscule; ces subtiles et terribles *mirettes*, que je reconnais à leur effrayante malice! Elles attirent, elles subjuguent, elles dévorent le regard de l'imprudent qui les contemple. Je les ai souvent étudiées, ces étoiles noires qui commandent la curiosité et l'admiration.

A quel démon bienveillant dois-je d'être ainsi entouré de mystère, de silence, de paix et de parfums? O béatitude! ce que nous nommons généralement la vie, même dans son expansion la plus heureuse, n'a rien de commun avec cette vie suprême dont j'ai maintenant connaissance et que je savoure minute par minute, seconde par seconde!

Non! il n'est plus de minutes, il n'est plus de secondes! Le temps a disparu; c'est l'Eternité qui règne, une éternité de délices!

Mais un coup terrible, lourd, a retenti à la porte, et, comme dans les rêves infernaux, il m'a semblé que je recevais un coup de pioche dans l'estomac.

Et puis un Spectre est entré. C'est un huissier qui vient me torturer au nom de la loi; une infâme concubine qui vient crier misère et ajouter les trivialités de sa vie aux douleurs de la mienne; ou bien le sauteruisseau d'un directeur de journal qui réclame la suite du manuscrit.

La chambre paradisiaque, l'idole, la souveraine des rêves, la *Sylphide*, comme disait le grand René, toute cette magie a disparu au coup brutal frappé par le Spectre.

Horreur! je me souviens! je me souviens! Oui! ce taudis, ce séjour de l'éternel ennui, est bien le mien. Voici les meubles sots, poudreux, écornés; la cheminée sans flamme et sans braise, souillée de crachats; les tristes fenêtres où la pluie a tracé des sillons dans la poussière; les manuscrits, raturés ou incomplets; l'almanach où le crayon a marqué les dates sinistres!

Et ce parfum d'un autre monde, dont je m'enivrais avec une sensibilité perfectionnée, hélas! il est remplacé par une fétide odeur de tabac melée à je ne sais quelle nauséabonde moisissure. On respire ici maintenant le ranci de la désolation.

Dans ce monde étroit, mais si plein de dégoût, un seul objet connu me sourit: la fiole de laudanum; une vieille et terrible amie; comme toutes les amies, hélas! féconde en caresses et en traîtrises.

Oh! oui! le Temps a reparu; le Temps règne en souverain maintenant; et avec le hideux vieillard est revenu tout son démoniaque cortège de Souvenirs, de Regrets, de Spasmes, de Peurs, d'Angoisses, de Cauchemars, de Colères et de Névroses.

Je vous assure que les secondes maintenant sont fortement et solennellement accentuéis, et chacune, en jaillissant de la pendule, dit:— "Je suis la Vie, l'insupportable, l'implacable Vie!"

Il n'y a qu'une Seconde dans la vie humaine qui ait mission d'annoncer une bonne nouvelle, la *bonne nouvelle* qui cause à chacun une inexplicable peur.

Oui! le Temps règne; il a repris sa brutale dictature. Et il me pousse, comme si j'étais un boeuf, avec son double aiguillon.—"Et hue donc! bourrique! Sue donc, esclave! Vis donc, damné!"

APPENDIX F

POISSON SOLUBLE no. 18

André Breton

Le réverbère qui se rapprochait insensiblement du bureau de poste cette nuit-là s'arrêtait à chaque instant pour prêter l'oreille. Est-ce à dire qu'il avait peur?

Dans l'établissement de bains, deux femmes très belles et sévèrement maquillées avaient retenu une heure auparavant la cabine la plus luxueuse et, comme elles s'attendaient à ne pas être seules, il avait été convenu qu'au premier signal (en l'espèce une fleur japonaise, de dimensions inaccoutumées, qui s'ouvrirait dans un verre d'eau) un alezan scellé se tiendrait derrière la porte. Cet animal piaffait superbement et le feu de ses naseaux jetait des araignées blanches sur les murs, comme lorsqu'on assiste à des tirs de marine lointains.

La foule allait et venait sur le boulevard sans rien connaître. De temps à autre elle se coupait les ponts, ou bien elle prenait à témoins les grands lieux géométriques de perle. Elle foulait une étendue qui pourrait être évaluée à celle des fraîcheurs autour des fontaines ou encore à ce que couvre d'illusions le manteau de la jeunesse, ce manteau de part en part troué par l'épée du rêve. Le réverbère évitait de se trouver pris dans la bousculade. A la hauteur de la porte Saint-Denis une chanson morte étourdissait encore un enfant et deux agents de la force publique : le "Matin" enchanté des buissons de ses linotypes, le café du Globe occupé par des lanciers quand ce n'est pas par des artistes de music-hall portées par le dédain.

Le paysage de Paris rossignol du monde variait de minute en minute et parmi les cires de ses coiffeurs élançait ses jolis arbres printaniers, pareils à l'inclinaison de l'âme sur l'horizon.

C'est alors que le réverbère, qui avait pris la rue Etienne-Marcel, jugea bon de s'arrêter et que je pus, passant par hasard comme un carton à dessin sous mon propre bras, surprendre une partie son monologue, tandis qu'il jouait de ruse pour ne pas arrêter l'autobus séduit par ses mains vertes, pareilles à un réseau de moustiques sur mes pas.

Le réverbère : "Sonia et Michelle feront bien de se méfier du rameau de fièvre qui garde les portes de Paris; l'évidence est qu'on ne fendra plus le bois de l'amour avant cette nuit. Si bien . . . si bien que je ne les vois pas blanches par ce printemps nocturne, pour peu que leur cheval prenne peur. Mieux vaudrait pour elles éviter la curiosité des lèvres, si elles succombent à la tentation des ponts jetés sur les regards. (Je vais les tracer.)"

Ce langage ne me causait aucune inquiétude encore quand le jour se mit à poindre, sous la forme d'un petit saltimbanque dont la tête était bandée et qui paraissait prêt à s'évanouir. L'enfant, après s'être appuyé négligemment au réverbère, se dirigea d'un trait vers la boîte des "Levées exceptionnelles" et, avant que j'eusse pu l'en empêcher, glissa fort avant son bras par l'ouverture. Je m'étais mis à attacher le lacet de mon soulier sur les marches quand il redescendit, plus mince que jamais, harassé de son effort, couvert de poussière et de plumes comme qui est tombé dans une haie, simple accident d'automobile dont on ne meurt pas toujours.

La chronologie de ces faits, des premiers au moins, chronologie à laquelle j'ai paru prendre une part inexplicable au début de ce récit, m'entraîne à ajouter que le timbre des instruments absents, Sonia et Michelle, était beaucoup plus sourd depuis que la lettre était partie. Elle ne devait, d'ailleurs, pas tarder à les rejoindre. En effet, dix minutes s'étaient à peine écoulées que j'entendis à nouveau une chemise, qui devait être verte, glisser lentement du dossier de la chaise de la cabine jusqu'à terre où elle vécut quelques temps de la vie d'un chardon, dans le sable, au bord de la mer. Le réverbère s'était transporté sur un boulevard de Dieppe où il s'efforçait d'éclairer un homme d'une quarantaine d'années occupé à chercher quelque chose dans le sable. Cet objet perdu j'aurais pu le lui montrer, puisque c'était un oeillet. Mais il allait et venait sans parvenir à le retrouver et je ne pus m'empêcher de sourire quand il jugea que ce manège avait assez duré et que, prenant une décision sauvage, il se mit à suivre la route de gauche, qui prolonge l'allée du casino. Michelle défit alors son bracelet et le posa sur le rebord de la fenêtre, qu'elle referma ensuite, après avoir considéré la trace charmante qu'il laissait sur sa peau. Cette femme, blonde, me parut assez froide de coeur et je la chassai longtemps devant moi comme une gazelle. Sonia, d'un acajou splendide, s'était depuis longtemps déshabillée et son corps était moulé dans la lumière du plus merveilleux lieu de plaisir que j'aie jamais vu. Ses regards étaient des serpentins verts et bleus au milieu desquels, mais continuellement brisé, spiralait même un serpentin blanc, comme une faveur spéciale qui m'eût été réservée. Elle chantait entre les barreaux de l'eau ces mots que je n'ai pas appris :

"Mort d'azur et de tempête fine, défais ces barques, use ces noeuds. Donne aux divinités le calme, aux humains la colère. Je te connais, mort de poudre et d'acacia, mort de verre. Je suis morte, moi aussi, sous les baisers."

L'appât des songes stimule maintenant les musiques de ma tête. Ces deux femmes m'ont appartenu tout un jour que je finissais ténébreusement d'être jeune. Et me voici, prophète à la tempe plus pure que les miroirs, enchaîné par les lueurs de mon histoire, couvert d'amours glaçantes, en proie aux fantasmagories de la baguette brisée et demandant que par pitié, d'un seul brillant final, on me ramène à la vie.

APPENDIX G

POISSON SOLUBLE no. 28

André Breton

Je venais d'encourir ma millième condamnation pour excès de vitesse. On n'a pas oublié la nouvelle : cette auto filant un soir à toute allure sur la route de Saint-Cloud, cette auto dont les voyageurs portaient des armures. Or je faisais partie de cette équipée anachronique qui mit aux prises l'ombre des arbres, l'ombre tournoyante de la poussière avec notre ombre de carriers blancs et funestes. Il y eut des sauts de rivières, je me rappelle, dont n'approche depuis en audace que l'entrée solennelle des hommes-cages dans le vestibule de l'hôtel Claridge, par une belle après-midi de février. Il y eut cette même promptitude dans le désastre que le jour où le *rayon*, découvert depuis, commença à balayer les plaines glacées de Russie, alors que Napoléon n'attendait que la lumière infra-rouge. Des sauts de rivières et des vols planés en plein Paris, dans une auto dont les occupants sont tout bardés de rêve! On alla beaucoup plus loin que Saint-Cloud, dans l'ombre de cette statue équestre dont certains mirent, d'ailleurs, toute leur vie à sortir. De quel châtaignier millénaire tentions-nous de faire le tour? Ici une châtaigne descend, elle fait mine de se laisser tomber et, s'arrêtant à quelques mètres du sol, demeure suspendue comme une araignée.

Quand elles levaient leur visière, je découvrais à deux de mes compagnes des yeux châtains. Les formes s'étaient depuis longtemps révélées, la forme d'ombrelle notamment, qui se couvre de ciel, la forme de bottine qui rassemble étroitement les fleurs, au passage d'une rue, sur un refuge. Quoique nous fussions certains de ne point toucher terre, les habitants avaient reçu ordre de rester chez eux. L'auto promenait maintenant ses mains gantées de caoutchouc sur les meubles de la chambre-Paris. (On sait que dans les palaces il ne saurait être question de numéroter les chambres, les appartements; pure question de luxe, par suite, que ces sortes de désignations.) Mais moi j'avais bien franchi le stade du luxe : je ne voulais m'arrêter qu'à la ville 34. Mes compagnons avaient beau m'opposer le risque de manquer d'air avant d'atteindre ce chiffre, je n'écoutais que mon remords, ce remords de vivre dont je n'ai jamais manqué l'occasion de faire confidence, même aux femmes à la visière baissée. C'est dans les faubourgs de la ville 26 que se produisit le miracle : une voiture qui venait en sens inverse de la nôtre et commença par écrire mon nom à l'envers dans un merveilleux paraphe de flamme vint nous heurter légèrement; le diable sait si elle allait moins vite que nous. C'est ici que mon explication, je le sais, sera de nature à ne satisfaire que les plus hautes consciences sportives de ce temps : *dans le temps il n'y a plus de droite ni de gauche*, telle fut la moralité de ce voyage. Les deux bolides blanc et vert, rouge et noir fusionnèrent terriblement et je ne me retrouve que passagèrement depuis, mort ou vif, me mettant moi-même à prix sur de grands écriteaux comme celui-ci, que sur tous les arbres je cloue du poignard de mon coeur.

BIBLIOGRAPHY

Apollinaire, Guillaume. *Calligrammes*. Paris: Gallimard, 1925.

Armstrong, Paul B. "The Conflict of Interpretation and Limits of Pluralism." *PLMA*, 98, No. 3 (May 1983), 341-352.

Arnaud, Noel, Francis Lacassin, and Jean Tortel. *Entretiens sur la Paralittérature*. Paris: Librairie Plon, 1970.

Balakian, Anna. *Literary Origins of Surrealism*. New York: King's Press, 1947.

Barthes, Roland. *Critique et Vérité*. Paris: Seuil, 1966.

_____. "Introduction à l'analyse structurale du récit." *Communications*, 8 (1966), 26-27.

_____. *Le Degré zéro de l'écriture*. Paris: Seuil, 1972.

_____. *L'Empire des signes*. Genève: Skira, 1970.

_____. *Le Plaisir du texte*. Paris: Seuil, 1973.

_____. *Mythologies*. Paris: Seuil, 1970.

_____. *S / Z*. Paris: Seuil, 1970.

Baudelaire, Charles. *Oeuvres*. Ed. Claude Pichois. Paris: Bibliothèque de la Pléiade, 1975.

Baudry, Jean-Louis. "Le Texte de Rimbaud (fin)." *Tel Quel*, 36 (1969), 33-53.

Beaujour, Michel. "Short Epiphanies: Two Contextual Approaches to the French Prose Poem." In *The Prose Poem in France*. Ed. Mary Ann Caws and Hermine Riffaterre. New York: Columbia University Press, 1983, pp. 39-59.

Benedikt, Michael. *The Prose Poem*. New York: Dell, 1976.

Benveniste, Emile. *Problèmes de linguistique générale*. Paris: Gallimard, 1966.

Bernard, Suzanne. *Le Poème en prose de Baudelaire jusqu'à nos jours*. Paris: Nizet, 1959.

Bloom, Harold. *The Anxiety of Influence: A Theory of Poetry*. New York: Oxford Univ. Press, 1975.

Breton, André. *Manifestes du Surréalisme*. Paris: Jean-Jacques Pauvert, 1962.

――――. *Nadja*. Paris: Gallimard, 1964.

――――. *Perspective cavalière*. Paris: Gallimard, 1970.

Chapelan, Maurice, *Anthologie du poème en prose*. Paris: René Juilliard, 1946.

Chrétien de Troyes. *Le Chevalier de la Charrette*. Ed. Jean Frappier. Paris: Champion, 1971.

Cohen, Jean. "Poésie et redondance." *Poétique*, 28 (1976), 413-22.

Cohn, Robert Greer. *The Poetry of Rimbaud*. Princeton: Princeton Univ. Press, 1973.

Coste, Didier. "Trois conceptions du lecteur et leur contribution à une théorie du texte littéraire." *Poétique*, 43 (1980), 354-71.

Courtès, Joseph. *Lévi-Strauss et les contraintes de la pensée mythique*. Paris: Monc, 1973.

Culler, Jonathan. "Convention and Meaning: Derrida and Austin." *New Literary History,* 13, No. 1 (1981), 15-30.

――――. "Literary Competence." In *Reader-Response Criticism: From Formalism to Post-Structuralism*. Ed. Jane P. Tompkins. Baltimore and London: Johns Hopkins Univ. Press, 1980, pp. 101-77.

――――. "Prolegomena to a Theory of Reading." In *The Reader in the Text: Essays on Audience and Interpretation*. Ed. Inge Crosman and Susan R. Suleiman. Princeton: Princeton Univ. Press, 1980, pp. 44-66.

Delas, Daniel, and Jacques Filliolet. *Linguistique et Poétique.* Paris: Larousse, 1973.

Deleuze, Gilles. *Logique du sens.* Paris: Editions de Minuit, 1969.

————. *Différence et répétition.* Paris: PUF, 1972.

Derrida, Jacques. *De la grammatologie.* Paris: Editions de Minuit, 1967.

————."La Différance." In *Théorie d'ensemble.* Paris: Seuil, 1968, pp. 41-66.

————. *La Dissémination.* Paris: Seuil, 1972.

————. *L'Ecriture et la différence.* Paris: Seuil, 1967.

————. *Marges de la philosophie.* Paris: Editions de Minuit, 1972.

Dumarsais-Fontanier. *Les Tropes.* Ed. Gérard Genette. Geneva: Slatkine Reprints, 1967.

Eco, Umberto. *Opera aperta.* Milano: Bompian, 1962.

————. *A Theory of Semiotics.* Bloomington and London: Indiana Univ. Press, 1979.

Ellman, Richard, and Robert O'Clair, eds. *The Norton Anthology of Modern Poetry.* New York and London: W. W. Norton and Company, 1973.

Entretiens de Francis Ponge avec Philippe Sollers. Paris: Gallimard-Seuil, 1970.

Fish, Stanley. "How Ordinary is Ordinary Language?" *New Literary History* 5 (1973), 41-54.

————. *Self-Consuming Artifacts.* Berkeley: Univ. of California Press, 1972.

Foucault, Michel. "Qu'est-ce qu'un auteur?" *Bulletin de la Société Française de Philosophie,* 63, No. 3 (1969), 73-104.

————. *Raymond Roussel.* Paris: Gallimard, 1963.

Freud, Sigmund. *Beyond the Pleasure Principle.* Trans. James Strachey. New York: Bantam Books, 1967.

————. *Standard Edition.* Trans. James Strachey. London: Hogarth Press, 1953-74.

Genette, Gérard. *Mimologiques.* Paris: Editions de Seuil, 1976.

Goux, Jean-Joseph. "Numismatiques." Part I. *Tel Quel,* 35 (1968), 64-89.

Green, André. "Répétition, Différence, Réplication." *Revue Française de Psychanalyse,* 3, XXXIV (1970), 461-501.

Greimas, Algirdas Julien. *Du sens.* Paris: Seuil, 1970.

————. *Sémantique structurale.* Paris: Larousse, 1966.

Hamon, Philippe. "Clausules." *Poétique,* 24 (1975), 495-526.

Hartman, Geoffrey. *Beyond Formalism.* New Haven: Yale Univ. Press, 1971.

Hérédia, José-Maria de. *Les Trophées.* Cambridge: Cambridge Univ. Press, 1946.

Hernadi, Paul. *Beyond Genre.* Ithaca: Cornell Univ. Press, 1972.

Holland, Norman. *5 Readers Reading.* New Haven and London: Yale Univ. Press, 1975.

Hrushovski, Benjamin. "The Meaning of Sound Patterns in Poetry: An Interaction Theory." *Poetics Today,* 2, No. 1 (1980), 39-56.

Hugo, Victor. *Notre-Dame de Paris.* Paris: Garnier-Flammarion, 1967.

Iser, Wolfgang. "The Reading Process: A Phenomenological Approach." In *Reader-Response Criticism: From Formalism to Post-Structuralism.* Ed. Jane P. Tompkins. Baltimore: Johns Hopkins Univ. Press, 1980.

Jacob, Max. *Cornet à Dés*. Paris: Gallimard, 1945.

Jakobson, Roman. *Essais de linguistique générale*. Paris: Editions de Minuit, 1963.

———. *Questions de poétique*. Paris: Seuil, 1973.

Jameson, Fredric. *The Prison-House of Language*. Princeton: Princeton Univ. Press, 1972.

Johnson, Anthony. "Anagrammatism in Poetry: Theoretical Preliminaries." *PTL: A Journal for Descriptive Poetics and Theory of Literature*, 2 (1977), 89-118.

Johnson, Barbara. *The Critical Difference: Essays in the Contemporary Rhetoric of Reading*. Baltimore and London: John Hopkins Univ. Press, 1980.

———. "Quelques conséquences de la différence anatomique des textes." *Poétique*, 28 (1976), 450-65.

Keats, John. *The Complete Works*. Ed. Nathan Haskell Dole. London and Boston: Virtue and Company, 1904.

Kristéva, Julia. *Polylogue*. Paris: Seuil, 1977.

———. "La Productivité dite texte." *Communications*, 11 (1968), 59-83.

———. *La Révolution du langage poétique*. Paris: Seuil, 1974.

Kritzman, Lawrence. "Learning to Read: Literary Competence and Structuralist Poetics." *Dispositio*, 4 (1977), 113-17.

Lacan, Jacques. *Ecrits*. Paris: Seuil, 1966.

———. "The Insistence of the Letter in the Unconscious." In *Structuralism*. Ed. Jacques Ehrmann. Garden City, NY: Anchor Books, 1970, pp. 101-37.

Lautréamont (Isidore Ducasse). *Oeuvres complètes*. Paris: Garnier-Flammarion, 1969.

Létoublon, Françoise. "Le Miroir et la boucle." *Poétique,* 53 (1983), 19-36.

Levin, Samuel R. *Linguistic Structures in Poetry.* The Hague: Mouton & Co., 1962.

Little, Roger. "Rimbaud's 'Sonnet'." *Modern Language Review,* 75, Part 3 (July 1980), 528-533.

Lisle, Leconte de. *Oeuvres complètes, Poèmes antiques.* Paris: Librairie Alphonse Lemerre, 1927.

Lotman, Youri. *La Structure du texte artistique.* Paris: Gallimard, 1973.

Lotringer, Sylvère. "Le 'Complexe' de Saussure." *Semiotext(e),* 2, No. 1 (1975), 90-112.

———. "Flagrant délire." *Semiotext (e) Saussure's Anagrams,* 2, No. 1 (1975), 7-14.

Lowrie, Walter, trans. *Repetition.* By Soren Kierkegaard. Princeton: Princeton Univ. Press, 1941.

Maeterlinck, Maurice. *Serres chaudes.* Bruxelles: Lacomblez, 1895.

Mallarmé, Stéphane. *Poésies.* Paris: Gallimard, 1945.

Man, Paul de. *Allegories of Reading.* New Haven: Yale Univ. Press, 1979.

Mauron, Charles. *Des Métaphores obsédantes au mythe personnel.* Paris: Corti, 1963.

Mehlman, Jeffrey. *Revolution and Repetition: Marx / Hugo / Balzac.* Berkeley: Univ. of California Press, 1977.

Miller, J. Hillis. "Ariadne's Thread: Repetition and the Narrative Line." *Critical Inquiry,* 3, No. 1 (1976), 55-77.

———. "Deconstructing the Deconstructors." *Diacritics,* 5 (1975), 24-31.

———. *Fiction and Repetition: Seven English Novels.* Cambridge: Harvard Univ. Press, 1982.

Milly, Jean. *La Phrase de Proust.* Paris: Larousse, 1975.

Morier, Henri. *Dictionnaire de poétique et rhétorique.* Paris: PUF, 1961.

Nadeau, Maurice. *History of Surrealism.* New York: Macmillan, 1965.

Nerval, Gérard de. *Les Filles de Feu.* Paris: Garnier-Flammarion, 1965.

———. *Oeuvres.* Ed. Henri Lemaitre. Paris: Garnier, 1966.

Peirce, Charles Sanders. *Collected Papers.* Cambridge: Harvard Univ. Press, 1931-1958.

Prince, Gerald. "Introduction to the Study of the Narratee." In *Reader-Response Criticism: From Formalism to Post-Structuralism.* Ed. Jane P. Tompkins. Baltimore: Johns Hopkins Press, 1980, pp. 7-25.

Rastier, François. *Essais de sémiotique poétique.* Paris: Larousse, 1972.

Raymond, Marcel. *De Baudelaire au Surréalisme.* Paris: José Corti, 1952.

Riffaterre, Michael. "Describing Poetic Structures: Two Approaches to Baudelaire's "Les chats." In *Structuralism.* Ed. Jacques Ehrmann. Garden City, NY: Anchor Books, 1970, pp. 188-230.

———. *Essais de stylistique structurale.* Paris: Flammarion, 1971.

———. "Interpretation and Undecidability." *New Literary History,* 12, No. 2 (1981), 227-42.

———. *La Production du texte.* Paris: Seuil, 1979.

———. "La Syllepse intertextuelle." *Poétique,* 4 (1979), 496-501.

———. *Semiotics of Poetry.* Bloomington and London: Indiana Univ. Press, 1978.

Rimbaud, Arthur. *Illuminations.* Ed. Albert Py. Geneva: Librairie Droz, 1967.

———. *Oeuvres.* Ed. Suzanne Bernard. Paris: Garnier, 1960.

Rimon-Kenon, Shlomith. "Paradoxical Status of Repetition." *Poetics Today,* 1, No. 4 (1979), 151-59.

Ronsard, Pierre. *Oeuvres complètes.* Ed. Gustave Cohen. Paris: Bibliothèque de la Pléiade, 1950.

Ruwet, Nicolas. *Langage, Musique, Poésie.* Paris: Seuil, 1973.

———. "Malherbe: Hermogène ou Cratyle?" *Poétique,* 42 (1980), pp. 195-224.

———. "Parallélismes et déviations en poésie." In *Langue, Discours, Société.* Ed. Julia Kristéva, Jean-Claude Milner, Nicolas Ruwet. Paris: Seuil, 1975, pp. 307-51.

Sabatier, Robert. *La Poésie du Moyen Age.* Paris: Editions Albin Michel, 1975.

Said, Edward W. *The World, The Text, and The Critic.* Cambridge: Harvard Univ. Press, 1983.

Saussure, Ferdinand de. *Cours de linguistique générale.* Paris: Payot, 1979.

Sollers, Philippe. "Niveaux sémantiques d'un texte moderne." In *Théorie d'ensemble.* Paris: Seuil, 1968.

Starobinski, Jean. *Les Mots sous les mots.* Paris: NRF, 1971.

Stevens, Wallace. *The Collected Poems of Wallace Stevens.* New York: Knopf, 1955.

Suleiman, Susan. "Redundancy and the Readable Text." *Poetics Today,* 1, III (Spring 1980), 119-142.

Todorov, Tzvetan. *Les Genres du discours.* Paris: Seuil, 1978.

————— . *Introduction à la littérature fantastique.* Paris: Seuil, 1970.

Valéry, Paul. *Oeuvres.* Ed. Jean Hytier. Paris: Bibliothèque de la Pléaide, 1957.

Waugh, Linda R. "The Poetic Function in the Theory of Roman Jakobson." *Poetics Today,* 2, No. 1 (1980), 57-82.